GUITAR REPAIR

By Irving Sloane
CLASSIC GUITAR CONSTRUCTION
GUITAR REPAIR

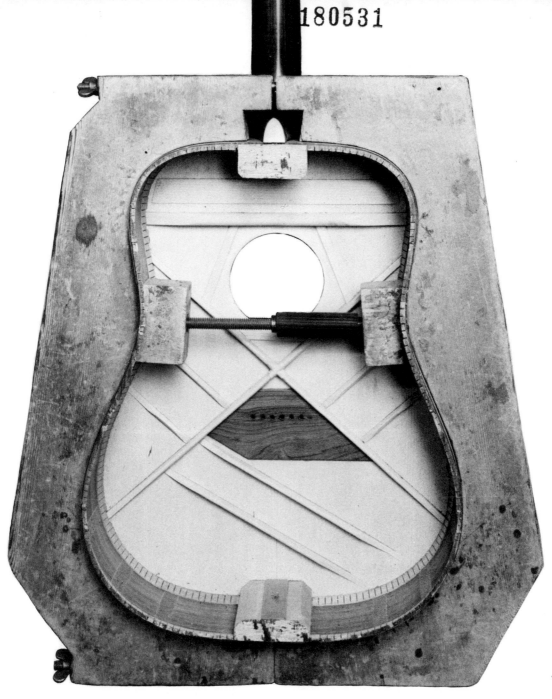

GUITAR REPAIR

A manual of repair for guitars and fretted instruments

IRVING SLOANE

E. P. DUTTON & CO., INC.

New York   *1973*

Published simultaneously in Canada by Clarke, Irwin & Company
Limited, Toronto and Vancouver
SBN: 0-525-12002-5

ACKNOWLEDGMENTS

This book is a companion volume to my earlier book, *Classic Guitar Construction,* and together they comprise a basic compendium of the most important aspects of guitar construction and repair. *Guitar Repair* came into being through the generous collaboration of the C. F. Martin Organisation and the many fine craftsmen who work there. Most of the photographs were taken at the Martin repair department in Nazareth, Pennsylvania, where the company honors without stint a warranty in effect since the days of Andrew Jackson's presidency—a record of corporate *noblesse* without parallel in the history of American business enterprise.

I owe a special debt to Donald Dech, a gifted craftsman who did all the splinting and patching sequences. Frank Loki, Paul Berger, Walter Lambert, Amazon Lahr, James Rampulla and the other men in the repair department gave important assistance at various stages of the book. Earl Remaley, Ray Bartholemew, Bob Fehr, and other supervisory personnel made things easy and typified the friendly courtesy that prevailed at all times.

The project began with the encouragement of John Huber, Technical Director of Martin, and relied extensively on his exhaustive knowledge of guitar construction and repair. His associate, Don Thompson, also provided help and technical information.

Garo Takoushian, a luthier with a special interest in the lute, did most of the restoration work on the Stautinger lute-guitar. Alberto Aroldi gave valuable photographic assistance.

I sincerely thank them all.

Irving Sloane

For
Christian Frederick Martin III

CONTENTS

INTRODUCTION

Stringed instruments are relatively fragile and more prone to damage than other kinds of musical instruments. Weather cycles of high humidity during warm summer months followed by rapid drying out in heated interiors during the winter time have a cumulative effect on wood and glue; wood is distorted and glue becomes weak. Added to this are the ordinary rigors of hard usage, while such mishaps as accidentally dropping the instrument, striking it or even inadvertently sitting down on it are not uncommon. A wooden instrument will also separate its seams if left in a closed case with the sun's rays baking down on it.

For all these reasons, a guitar is apt to keep repairmen busy at fairly regular intervals during its lifetime. The most basic problems are poor action, buzzing, cracks and fractures, loose bridge and worn finish. Essentially the same problems are found in the mandolin, ukelele, and to some degree in the banjo and lute, so that many of the procedures described in this book are applicable to these instruments. However, with the exception of repair of cracks, the methods given here do not apply to violins and other members of the viol family, where special techniques are required for repair.

The principal instrument used here to demonstrate repair techniques is the traditional hollow-bodied acoustic guitar, also known as the Spanish or folk guitar, strung with either nylon or metal strings depending on the style of construction. Nylon-strung guitars have a bridge with pierced tie block through which the strings are first threaded and then secured. Metal-strung flat-top guitars employ a bridge with removable pegs. The ball ends of the strings are dropped into holes drilled through the bridge and into the interior of the guitar. The pegs are then replaced, jamming and holding the string ends in place. Guitars with metal strings usually have a hardwood reinforcing plate glued to the underside of the soundboard where the bridge is located, to counter the stronger pull and tension of steel strings. Metal strings must never be used on a guitar built for nylon strings.

Factory-built guitars made in the United States differ widely in quality but not in the essential details of their manufacture. They all use a violin-type dovetailed key joint to join the neck to the body. This permits complete fabrication of the body before attaching the neck. Classic guitars built in the Spanish tradition use an integrated neck that joins to the sides before the

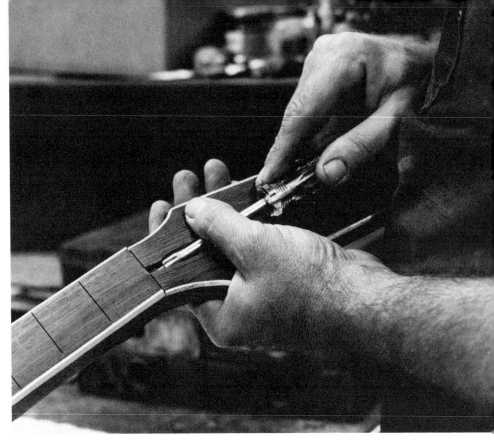

1. Tightening adjustable truss rod

soundboard and back are glued on, an excellent method but one that is impractical for modern factory production.

Imported guitars have flooded the U.S. market, notably from Japan. The cheaper models are made of plywood to minimize the hazard of cracking, the nightmare of all manufacturers faced with the problem of shipping their guitars to countries with widely different climates. But while plywood guitars do not crack as easily as solid wood guitars, they suffer all the other ills to which guitars are prone and generally have an inferior tone.

In the steel-string guitar, where the considerable tension of the strings subjects a neck to greater strain than the neck of a nylon-string guitar, American manufacturers use a steel truss rod or other rigid metal bar to reinforce the neck and combat the possibility of warping. The rod is set into a channel grooved in the top face of the neck before the fretboard is attached. In some models these rods can be adjusted with a key or wrench to counteract neck warp. Instructions for the adjustment of these rods can be had from the manufacturers.

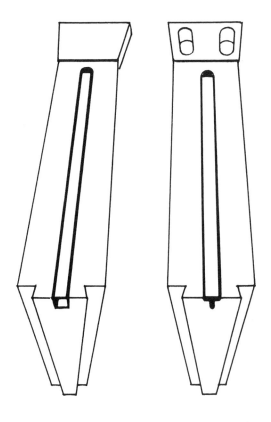

2. Channel bar and T-bar neck reinforcement

3. Martin D-18, D-28, D-35 (steel strings)

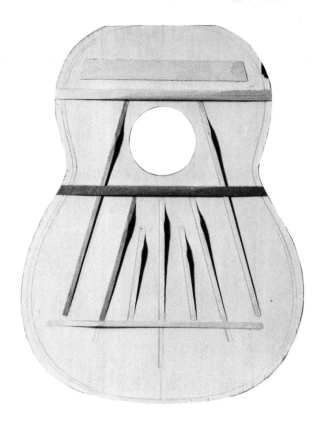

4. Martin N-10, N-20 (nylon strings)

Soundboard bracing patterns for steel-string guitars vary only slightly from one make to another, the guiding principle being strength. Bracing patterns in nylon-string guitars run a broader gamut of design and are more acoustically oriented.

The standard finish for commercially produced guitars is several coats of spray lacquer buffed to a gloss finish with an electric buffing machine and lacquer polishing compound. The refinishing techniques described on pages 88-93 include this method as well as the use of varnish and hand polishing.

Experienced woodworkers will have no problem in mastering the techniques of guitar repair. Those with guitar building experience will find repair work a natural extension of their building skills. But beyond the ordinary considerations of craftsmanship there are other, more subtle aspects of *lutherie*—the art of building and repairing stringed instruments—that unfold with experience.

Like lovers of fine wine, luthiers and players of long

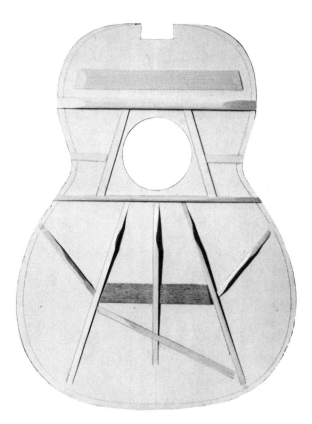

5. Martin 00-16C, 00-18C, 00-28C (nylon strings)

experience go through a familiar ritual when judging a fine guitar. First, the guitar is hefted for weight and balance. The craftsmanship of rosette, purflings, head detail, heel, and bridge are noted. Particular attention is paid to the soundboard grain, checking annular divisions for narrow, uniform striation and the crossgrain "silking" pattern that denotes the hardness and temper favored by the great guitar makers. All of these visual impressions precede the initial sounding of the instrument.

An air of expectancy and suspense accompany the first tentative notes as the luthier's fingers move from low to high register testing the action and musical balance. Slowly, an impression builds of the musical quality of the instrument. A final, somewhat mystical question remains—is all the sound coming out of the sound box or only a portion?

The promise inherent in excellent wood and beautiful craftsmanship is not always realized by the sound that issues from the box. Something is missing. Perhaps the bass is rich, resonant, but the treble is thin, insubstantial. Can it be the bracing? Or the thickness of the top?

Such judgments about the fullness of sound and purely musical qualities of a guitar are entirely subjective, of course, and measurable only in terms of one's experience with many guitars. The cultivation of this kind of critical "ear" is an important part of the process of learning to build and repair guitars.

Custom-made guitars are expensive and the supply of customers for such instruments is always small. Repair work is the bread-and-butter kind of activity that even the most celebrated luthiers have found necessary for economic survival. There are many good guitar makers but first-class repairmen are discouragingly hard to find.

6. *Tools of the luthier*

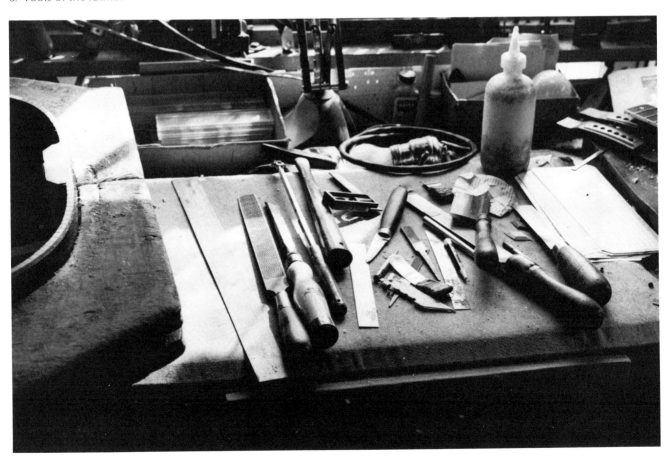

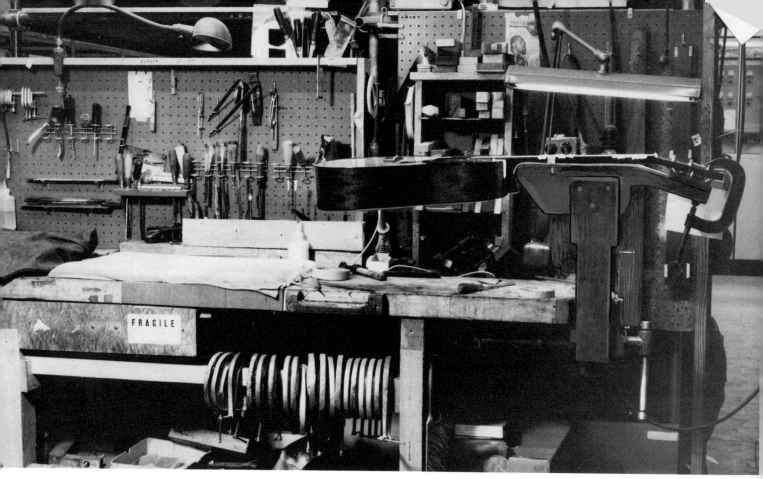

7. *Typical work bench with guitar clamped in felt-lined cradle affixed to rigid upright support*

WORK AREA

Ideally, the work bench should be situated near a large window that gathers north light. Auxiliary overhead lighting should be bright enough to illumine all parts of the work area. For close-up work, attach a small goose-neck or flexible arm lamp to the back of the work bench. Electric outlets, at least two, conveniently close to the bench are needed for work lamp, heat lamp, sander, buffer, and soldering iron.

Heavyweight felt, the kind favored by wood finishers for padding, is the ideal protective material for covering the main work area of the bench. It has just the right resilience and nap for guitar repair. A suitable substitute can be made using a quilted mattress pad with an outer covering of felt. Polyurethane foam-textile laminates or foam-rubber carpet cushion (solid not waffle) can also be used with an outer covering of felt. A soft, springy work pad is to be avoided. It is exasperating to use a chisel on a guitar and find that the guitar moves under each cut in response to the spongy nature of the work pad. A small felt-padded block is usually placed next to a stop at one end of the work area to accommodate the head of the guitar and keep it from shifting.

Along the back of the bench arrange a space to store your files, scrapers, chisels, nippers, and all other tools within plain view and easy reach. Instrument repairers should cultivate the habit of keeping their work area tidy and uncluttered. A careful inspection of the work area should be made each time before you lay down an instrument. An unnoticed fragment of fret wire or a large speck of ebony can cause damage that will necessitate additional repair work.

Adjacent counter space is always useful as well as shelves for storing wood. No decent-sized scrap of wood salvaged from a damaged guitar should be discarded. Builders of guitars should mark and store the waste portions of top and backs. The purchaser of the guitar will be heartened by the knowledge that his luthier can make an exact match if piecing-in a splint becomes necessary, and the luthier himself will save a great deal of tedious matching time.

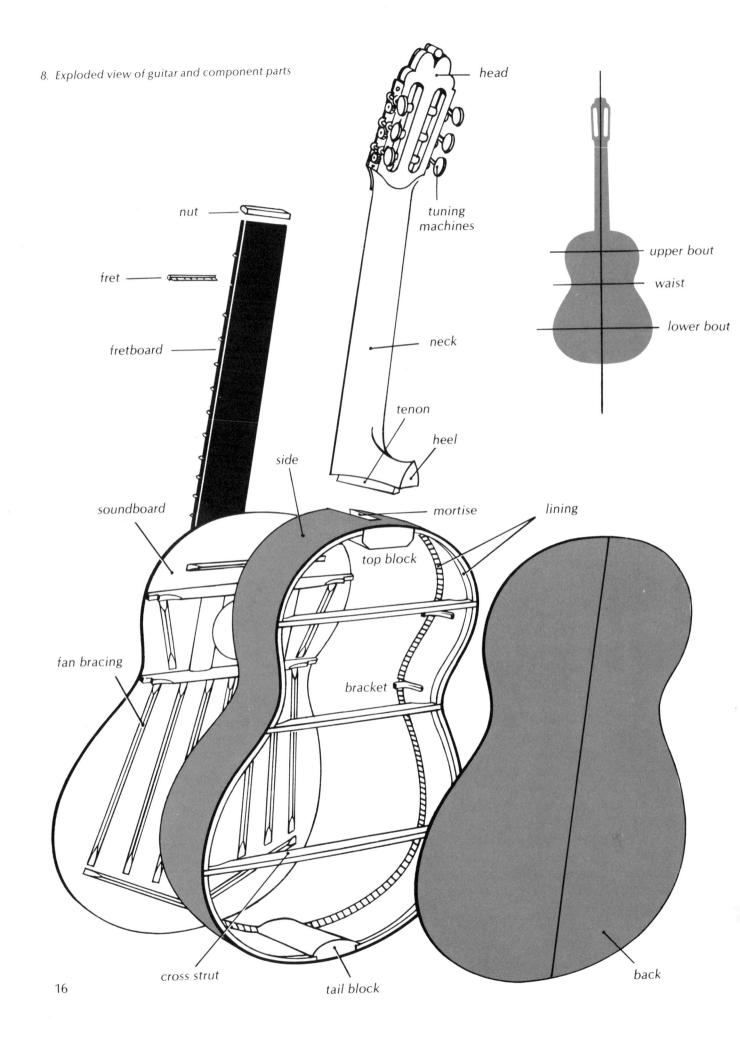

head

tuning machines

nut

fret

fretboard

neck

tenon

heel

side

mortise

lining

soundboard

top block

fan bracing

bracket

cross strut

tail block

back

upper bout

waist

lower bout

16

WOOD, SUPPLIES

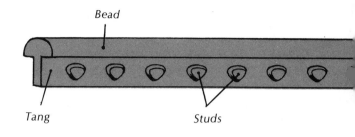

A good supply of wood is indispensable for expert repair work. All the skill in the world will not compensate for a mismatched piece of wood. Spruce soundboard wood should be carefully sorted as to color, grain, and general character. Portions of this reserve should be exposed to sunlight for varying lengths of time to ensure a good supply of top wood with the color that only sun aging can give it.

It is particularly important to collect and store Brazilian rosewood. Recent restrictions on the export of rosewood logs by the Brazilian government have forced guitar manufacturers to switch their production to East Indian rosewood, which is different in both color and density. Guitars of quality manufacture and almost all custom-made guitars have until recently been made of Brazilian rosewood. For many years, at least, a considerable portion of repair work will involve rosewood guitars, so wood for splints and patches must be stockpiled.

Fret wire (Fig. 9) comes in several gauges. The studded tang changes thickness but the fret bead remains the same. Refretting tends to enlarge fret slots and it is important to have a supply of different thicknesses to ensure a tight, secure anchoring of fret replacements.

Ivory nuts and saddles of different heights and thicknesses come in handy when all the guitar needs is raising the string height to adjust the action. Flat pieces of mother-of-pearl are useful for replacing lost marquetry or inlay.

Finally, an up-to-date file of the catalogs and listings of guitar and instrument parts suppliers (page 95) will provide ready access to needed parts and supplies.

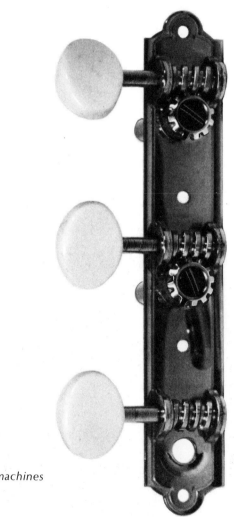

10. Single unit and multiple tuning machines

GLUE

Almost all the repair work described in this book is done with white polyvinyl resin glue sold commonly as Elmer's Glue. To glue on tops and backs, hide glue is recommended to facilitate future removal of these parts. Hide glue is also kinder to the cutting edges of the high speed router bits used to remove the corner ledge for bindings. White glues tend to build a gummy residue on hot cutter edges that will cause overheating.

Bridge, neck joint, splints, and even cracks are glued with white glue. Plastic bindings will not glue well with white glue and should be glued with Duco Cement instead.

In ordinary workroom temperatures white glue sets quickly, dries clear, and holding power is very good. A fretboard attached with polyvinyl resin glue can be easily removed through the use of a heat lamp (Fig. 19) because of the white glue's thermoplastic properties.

Animal or hide glue made from the hooves, bones, sinews, and skin linings of cattle has been the staple adhesive of instrument makers for hundreds of years. This glue is manufactured in different grades of varying strength and comes in sheet, flake, chip, or granular form.

To prepare animal glue, place the glue in a double-jacket glue pot with enough cold water to cover and leave to soak. When the glue has absorbed as much water as it can hold, the glue pot is heated to a temperature that must not exceed 150° F, a hazard that can be circumvented with an electric glue pot.

The best grades of hide glue prepared in this manner are strong and dependable. For optimum results the glue must be freshly made to the right consistency and temperature. Repeated diluting and reheating weakens the glue. Gluing must be done in a warm room with the work to be glued also heated so that clamps can be applied before the glue jells.

Liquid hide glue is also available in ready-to-use form. It is in many respects similar to hot glue but with a slower setting time, permitting ample time for coating and assembly before clamping.

11. Carefully gluing segmented abalone shell inlay with 3M Scotch Grip

12. *Work light and mirror*

TOOLS

In addition to the ordinary complement of chisels, files, clamps, and such, specialized tools are used in the repair of guitars and other stringed instruments. Some of these more highly specialized tools appear as a photographic footnote in the chapters where they are used, but there are a few tools whose usage in repair work is so common that they are listed here at the outset:

> *Work light and flexible mirror*
> *Fret slot saws*
> *Deep-throat clamps*
> *Clock-spring probes, spatulas*
> *Box clamps*
> *Wooden jacks*
> *Metal scraper blades*
> *Fretting hammer*
> *Block plane*
> *Long-handled glue scraper*

Some of these tools are available from supply houses, the rest are homemade. A work light can easily be assembled and uses a small bulb of no more than 10 watts. Mainspring wire from an old alarm clock provides the basic material for a most important repair tool. A piece of this wire makes a thin, supple blade that, when attached to a makeshift handle, becomes a fine probe. Such probes are used to separate narrow glue joints and search out crevices that might exist under loose braces and supports. A useful assortment would include a small one for separating or penetrating the glue joint of bindings; a large one for prying off fretboards and bridges; a curved one for checking the glue joint of braces and supports.

Art-supply stores sell large, whippy spatulas that are useful for separating plates (top and back) from the sides. If clock-spring wire is not at hand, these spatulas can be cut down and made into excellent probes. Care must be taken in sharpening these probes to avoid giving them a knife-edge sharpness. They are not supposed to cut and should only be thinned. Also avoid grinding these blades since heat can damage their temper and suppleness.

Wooden jacks are used to lift or rock a crack section to permit glue to enter the furthest recesses of the crack. Jacks are easily jigsawed out of pine, birch,

*Clock-spring wire made into
probes with winding of tape
for simple handle*

*Broad spatula made from scraper
blade and used for lifting fretboards*

Deep-throat flip clamp

Box clamp

Block plane

CRAFTSMAN 107-37088

13. Commonly used tools in guitar repair

Chasing hammer for fretting

gumwood, or any other wood. A few different sizes are needed to handle different interior depths. Sand them smooth and coat with shellac or varnish.

Box clamps are simple to make using threaded steel stock and 3/4″ plywood. Glue two sheets of plywood together and bandsaw them to shape. Drill a hole through the end of the top arm and screw a plate with threaded hole over the bottom exit of the drill hole. Two box clamps would serve for most purposes but it is better to have four. They weigh a fraction of what steel C-clamps of comparable jaw width weigh, provide more than adequate clamping pressure, and rest conveniently on a flat bottom. For those interested in making box clamps with threaded wooden parts, a wood threading kit is available from Woodcraft Supply Corp., Woburn, Mass.

Long-handled glue scrapers are designed to reach every interior spot in a guitar. They are simply slender steel rods with a small scraping blade welded to one end. Guided by means of a mirror, they are used to scrape away excess glue from inside surfaces that cannot be reached with the hand.

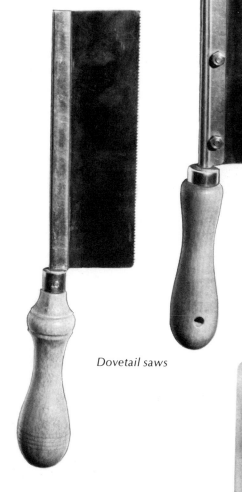

Dovetail saws

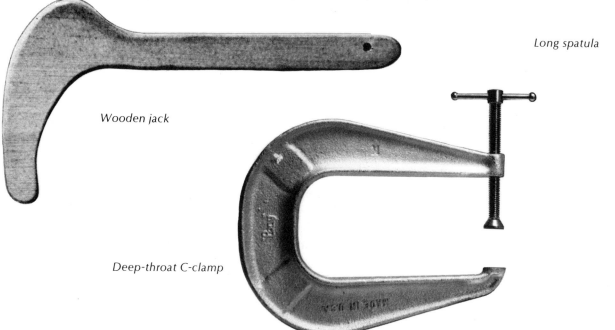

Wooden jack

Deep-throat C-clamp

Long spatula

14. Polished end of old file used as burnisher

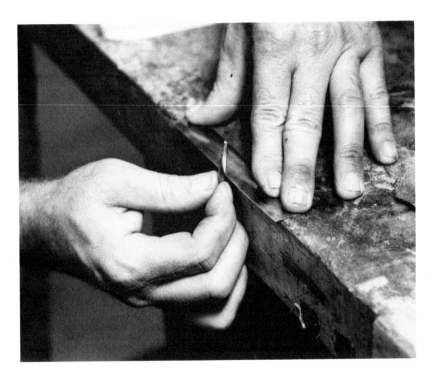

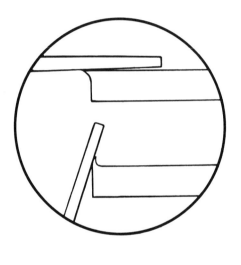

15. After drawing the edge, it is turned over into a long cutting burr

Metal scraper blades are handy for removing wood in places where it is impossible or awkward to use a plane. The trick in using them is knowing how to "turn an edge." The long edges must be honed dead flat and square by sliding the blade over a sharpening stone, using a wooden block to keep it perfectly vertical. The blade is then laid on its side and honed until the edge is knife-edge square. Position the blade on the edge of the work bench and draw a steel burnisher across the flat face of the blade along the edge. Do this once or twice to draw the edge which you then turn over by running the burnisher across the thin edge at a slight angle.

HUMIDITY

Since most of the problems that beset stringed instruments have their origin in alternating extremes of dampness and dryness and the accompanying expansion and contraction, it is important that workshop humidity be controlled. Instruments brought into the workshop for repair should remain undisturbed for at least a week to dispel excess moisture in the wood. Gluing shut a crack in a "wet" guitar before a suitable drying-out period will substantially increase the probability of a subsequent reopening of the crack during a dry period.

Stringed instruments should be built and repaired in an atmosphere containing less moisture than the atmosphere in which they will most commonly be used, since swelling—the absorption of atmospheric moisture—is a less serious hazard than shrinkage. For this reason, it is always best to build or work on wooden instruments in a relatively dry environment.

The critical surfaces for expansion and contraction in a guitar are the top and back. The end grain—easiest point of entry for atmospheric moisture—is sealed off by the binding. Absorption of moisture is further retarded by the varnish or other protective finish. If the guitar has been carefully made and properly braced, the problem of swelling is not great. The most scrupulous craftsmanship, however, will count for little in the face of an abrupt, serious loss of moisture and the resultant deformation of wood. Sudden drying out of wooden instruments is the major cause of cracks and seam separation.

Ideally, the percentage of relative humidity in the workshop should fall between 45% and 55%. A good hygrometer (a device for measuring percentage of relative humidity) is an important investment. Hang it on a wall away from doors and windows. Excessive dryness—percentages below 30%—can be helped by the use of plants, trays of water, or an electric humidifying device. Never store wooden instruments near sources of heat or moisture.

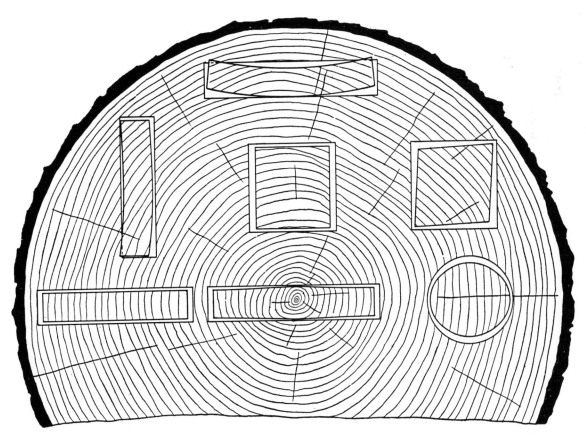

16. *Characteristic shrinkage and distortion of flats, squares, and rounds as affected by the direction of the annual rings*

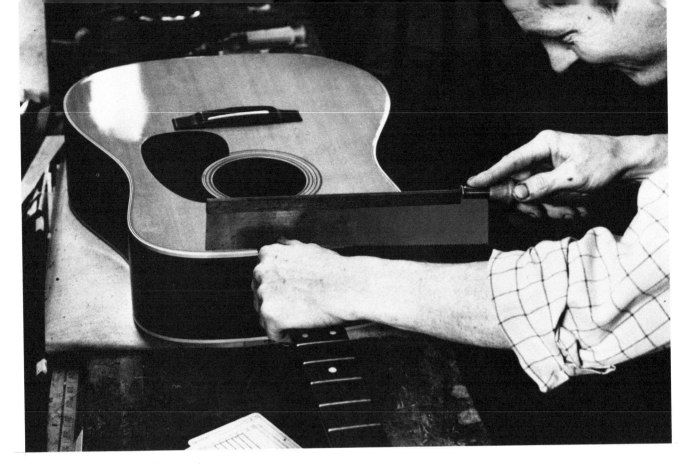

17. Sawing through twelfth fret slot

18. Lifting heated fretboard with broad spatula

WARPED NECK

An obvious sign that a neck is warped is the increased difficulty of fingering because of the enlarged gap between frets and strings. A quick check with a long straightedge will reveal any misalignment. If there is no sign of separation or movement where the contoured heel fits against the back, the neck is probably warped. If the heel has separated, the neck may simply be tilted and not warped. In any case, distortion of the neck for any protracted period will also warp the fretboard.

Necks that are only bowed to a slight degree can sometimes be brought back into line by just installing a new fretboard. Warped necks can also be straightened by making use of the wedging action of oversized frets (see Refretting, page 37) or by removing the frets and planing the fretboard level. Planing, obviously, is a remedy that cannot be used to correct a serious condition. A seriously warped neck must be reset or replaced

Removal of the neck begins with removal of the lower portion of the fretboard that is glued to the soundboard. Factory-built guitars have a dovetailed key joint (Fig. 2) that is exposed by removing this part of the fretboard. Classic or flamenco guitars that use an integrated neck do not have a key joint and removing the neck involves virtual dismemberment of the guitar. If an integrated neck must be replaced it can be sawed off next to the body and a key joint neck installed.

Begin by lifting the fret wire at the twelfth fret or whichever fret coincides with the juncture of body and neck. Saw down through the fret slot with a fine dovetail saw until the fretboard is severed. Scribe a fine line in the top around the fretboard to mark its position. Use a fine-pointed metal scriber, pressing just hard enough to scratch the finish but not the wood.

Jigsaw a sheet of asbestos into a mask that will protect the soundboard from the direct rays of a heat lamp (Fig. 19). Suspend a heat lamp about 8" from the fretboard and heat for about 5 minutes. Remove the lamp and mask and quickly insert a broad spatula into the glue joint beneath the fretboard. Work the spatula from both sides until the fretboard comes away. If enough heat has not reached the glue to soften it, reheat.

When this portion of the fretboard has been removed the top entrance of the key joint will be exposed. Leak a few drops of hot water into the glue joint around the key or dovetail. A syringe or hypodermic

19. *Heating fretboard masked with asbestos*

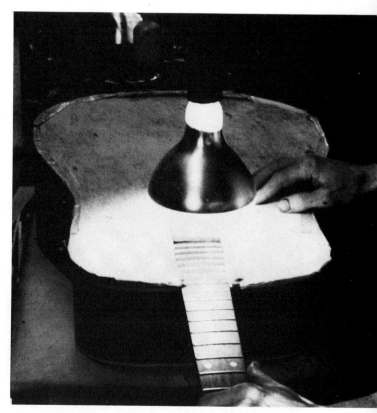

20. Cleaning sides of tenon

21. Filing down shimmed sides of mortise

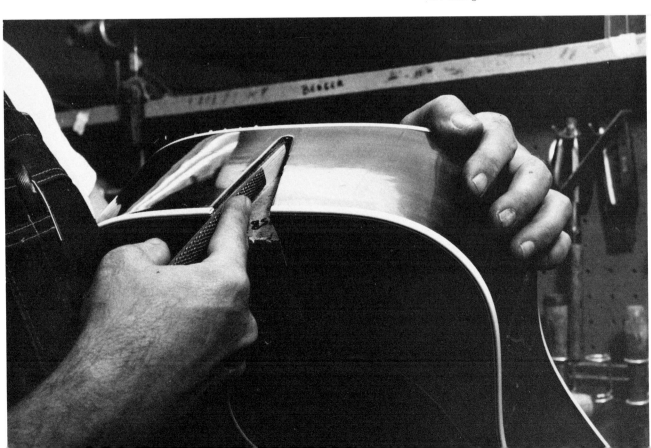

22. Lining up neck with two strings

needle is a fine tool for getting hot water into such glue joints. Allow the water to soak into the joint for an hour. Grip the guitar near the head and try to rock the neck. Insert a slim probe into the key joint and use some more hot water until the key begins to move in the joint. Try to work it loose without hammering on the heel, a form of shock treatment that may crack the heel.

Clean all the old glue from the gluing surfaces of both the dovetail and mortise. File smooth these surfaces and with the guitar resting on a level surface, reinsert the key in the mortise. Rock the neck to determine where play exists in the joint. If the neck tilts up

and down there is play in the frontal faces of the joint. Side-to-side motion indicates play in the lateral faces. Shims made of thin veneer sections will have to be glued to the faces of the mortise to eliminate play. And these faces may have to be filed down to make room for the shims.

Attach strings to the first and last holes in the bridge. Lead them over their respective grooves in the nut and use them as a guide for longitudinal alignment of the neck. Use a straightedge long enough to reach from the top of the fretboard to the bridge saddle to check the horizontal realignment of the neck. The main purpose of resetting the neck is to bring the head back

23. Long centering rule to check alignment when bridge is off

24. *Scraping old glue from fretboard gluing area*   25. *Clamping arrangement for bottom end of fretboard*

down into horizontal alignment. By testing, removing, filing, and testing again, keep adjusting the neck until the key joint fits snugly with the top surface of the neck in the same plane as the soundboard.

In those cases where the neck is simply tilted because the key joint is loose, the neck will come out easily once the fretboard has been severed at the body joint. If the fretboard appears to be in good shape, do not sever the fretboard at the body juncture. Leave the entire fretboard intact so that it will come off with the neck when the bottom section of the fretboard has been freed.

If the fretboard has to be removed from the neck, scrape away the finish that covers the long glue joint on both sides of the neck. Use the heat lamp, judiciously applied moisture, and a spatula or heated knife to separate the fretboard from the neck.

Prepare a new fretboard to replace the old one. Trim and smooth it until it is an exact copy of the original. Saw the slots but do not lay in the fret wires. Carefully position the new fretboard on the neck in the position occupied by the old fretboard and glue it.

Fit the neck-fretboard assembly back into the key

joint, using the two strings and long straightedge to check alignment. When everything checks out—the joint is snug, the alignment true, and the fretboard lies tight against the soundboard—remove the assembly and apply white glue to the key and mortise surfaces with a small paintbrush. Also coat the bottom of the fretboard with glue and quickly reinsert the assembly. Wipe away all glue ooze with a damp cloth. Using an inner and outer caul, position a clamp through the sound hole, lightly gripping the fretboard. Check the alignment again with the two strings and tighten the clamp when alignment is perfect. Complete the clamping of the neck and fretboard to the body, as shown.

If the lower half of the fretboard was severed, clean all glue from the back and glue it back in the area delineated by the scribed outline. Check with feeler gauge and fret with the appropriate gauge of fret wire.

No matter how precisely these corrective procedures are followed, the need for critical judgment and good sense still exists. One procedure may be enough to do the job or a combination of all three—fretboard planing, oversized fret-wedging technique, neck resetting—may have to be used.

26. *Wiping away glue ooze after clamping key joint*

27. *Twelve-string pin bridge*

ACTION and BUZZING

Action is a term that defines the quality of a guitar's playability. A stiff or hard action means fingering will require a forceful, positive attack; a soft or fast action means that fingering can be lighter and more rapid. Flamenco players prefer an unusually fast action, so fast that an occasional buzz caused by the close proximity of strings to fretboard is an acceptable defect. Classical guitarists prefer a stiffer action that demands a more disciplined attack and delivers a cleaner sound projection.

Action is determined by both the distance of the strings from the frets and the string tension. The more tension on a string, the more force will be required to set the string in motion. Similarly, increasing the distance between strings and frets will increase the pressure needed to finger a note or chord.

Action is a crucial concern for the player. It hardly matters how magnificent a guitar sounds if it is impossible to play. An important distinction that separates good guitars from bad ones is the quality of the action. Cheap, mass-produced guitars are often difficult to play because the action has been standardized at unnecessarily stiff levels to foreclose the possibility of buzzing—sudden death to a guitar sale. In well-made guitars individual attention is given to the action of each instrument to ensure that playability is not impaired. Hermann Hauser, the great German luthier, was obsessed with action. On many guitars he purposely lowered the bass side of the fingerboard between the seventh and twelfth frets to make possible a relatively easy action without the risk of bass string buzz or slap—the last stage in bass string excursion after being set in motion with uncommon force.

An easy, natural action can only be achieved if the fingerboard is true with all frets properly aligned and the correct amount of space between frets and strings from the top nut to bridge saddle. Adjustment of action proceeds by first tuning the guitar to concert pitch. Twelve-string guitars are usually pitched lower and most of them, in fact, cannot be tuned to concert pitch without dire consequence to the neck and bridge. If a player normally pitches his guitar lower, then the action will have to be regulated at this level.

Usually, raising or lowering the nut or saddle is all that need be done to improve an action if the fretboard is true. In grooving a nut, allowance must be made for

the thicker gauge of bass strings. Also, the gap between bass strings and frets is always greater than on the treble side to allow for bass string excursion—an effect similar to cracking a whip. Bass strings are not under as high a tension as treble strings and this slackness makes possible a greater excursion when the string is set in motion. Slapping may not occur unless the bass string—E string usually—is set in motion with considerable force. Again, individual usage is involved. A player with a light attack is not likely to cause bass slap while flamenco players with their powerful use of the thumb for rapid passages are more likely to do so. The luthier must take such considerations into account and regulate the action accordingly. Strings are available in high or low tension and can be selected to improve action but the difference in tension is not great enough to correct serious deficiencies in action.

Buzzing, by far the most common complaint, is traceable to a number of causes. In their order of probable frequency, they are:

Loose or misaligned fret
Nut or bridge saddle too low; defective nut
Bad string
Loose brace
Warped neck
Channel-bar vibration
Resonating dissonance

Begin the search by first checking tuning machines to make sure no part is loose or vibrating. A loose button will vibrate at certain frequencies, emitting a buzzing noise.

The fastest way of spotting a bad fret is by sighting

28. Sight down fretboard to locate loose fret

down the fretboard. The constant shrinkage and expansion of the fretboard occasionally will dislodge a fret. To check further, hold a steel straightedge or rule against the fret. Finally, starting at the top, finger each consecutive fret on a buzzing string until the buzzing stops. The fret following the one where no buzzing occurs is the likely culprit.

Hammering in a dislodged fret is at best a temporary remedy and it is always better to remove it and install a thicker gauge of fret wire. (See Refretting, page 37.)

When the nut or saddle is too low, buzzing is general over a wide range and will affect several or all strings. This condition is easy to spot and can be promptly corrected by raising the nut or saddle. If the frets check out true and the neck is not warped, then the saddle should be raised slightly. String clearance is measured at the fret that falls over the body joint—twelfth or fourteenth fret—and is measured from the bottom of the string to the top of the fret wire. Recommended clearances for the treble E string and the bass E string are:

Steel-string acoustic: $3/32''$ *treble,* $4/32''$ *bass*
Nylon-string: $4/32''$ *treble,* $5/32''$ *bass*

These are industry standards but individual guitar makers often work nylon-string tolerances down to $4/64''$ treble and $5/64''$ bass.

Loosen the strings and raise the saddle by inserting a thin veneer shim under it. Try this before changing the nut. If this doesn't do the job, a slightly thicker shim may have to be tried to achieve a buzz-free action. When the exact height of saddle or nut has been ascertained through the use of shims, a new saddle and nut cut to the new height should be installed. Both saddle and nut must be cut to fit snugly in place with their bottom edges in solid contact with the floor of their grooves.

A nut can cause string buzz if the string grooves get rounded to the point where the string is actually being stopped on top of a ridge in the groove. If the string is not being cleanly stopped at the front face of the nut, buzzing can occur. Cut a new nut with the top edge beveled so that the string grooves slant down toward the head of the guitar. File the grooves with a jeweler's rat-tail file and make them just wide enough to hold the string.

If the buzz is recent and has not occurred in previous stringings, a bad string or loose brace should be suspected. Bad strings give a flat, tubby sound that will buzz in several or all positions and make tuning the guitar difficult. The clearest sign of a bad string is a corroded or tarnished winding or a string that has gone out of round (feel it). Installing a new set of strings is the fastest way of eliminating a bad string as a possible cause of buzzing.

When a brace is loose, buzzing will normally occur at a specific pitch or pitches. Tapping the soundboard will sometimes make a loose brace vibrate if the tap is on top of or very close to the loose section. The surest way of tracking down a loose brace is with a light-and-mirror inspection of the bracing. Insert the light and mirror into the guitar and move the soundboard with your free hand; press and release the top while examining the braces. If visual inspection does not turn up the brace separation, then inspection must be continued with a probe. For repair of a loose brace see page 62, Loose Braces.

Buzzing is rarely caused by neck warp. Necks, with or without truss rods, are fairly rigid and neck warp is not as common as one might imagine. Usually, neck warp occurs through the lifting upward of the head of the guitar by excessive string tension over a long period of time. When this happens the strings move further away from the fretboard, making fingering of high notes very difficult. For buzzing to occur, the neck would have to cant downward, bringing the strings closer to the fretboard. A prominent cause of this sort of warping is the improper adjustment of adjustable truss rods. A truss rod that is tightened excessively when atmospheric humidity is abnormally low (a heated room in winter) will force a neck out of wind—diagonal distortion—when the humidity reaches wilting levels. A neck that is permanently distorted in this way must be replaced with a new neck.

Buzzing caused by channel-bar vibration can be isolated by tapping the neck. Bars are glued into a channel grooved into the top face of the neck. If they work loose in their groove, they will rattle when the neck is smartly tapped. Bar rattle can sometimes be eliminated by removing the pearl dots set into the face of the fretboard. Pry them loose with the point of a sharp knife and drill down through the hole with a drill

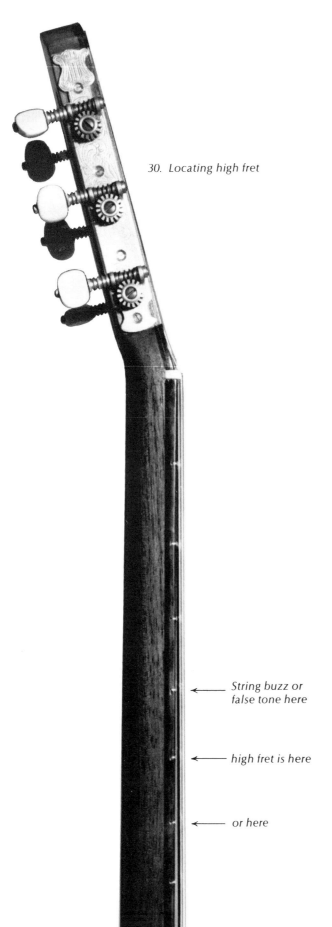

30. Locating high fret

String buzz or false tone here ←

high fret is here ←

or here ←

smaller than the hole's diameter until the bar is reached. Inject glue into the hole with an ear syringe that has been trimmed back to the point where the nozzle fits snug in the hole. If the glue seeps into the right crannies, it will harden and stop the rattling. This usually works but if it doesn't, the fretboard will have to come off (Warped Neck, page 25). With the fretboard removed, the bar is completely exposed and it is a simple matter to fill all crevices with glue or reglue the bar if it is completely loose.

Channel-rod and truss-rod rattle is a relatively rare phenomenon except in the case of adjustable truss rods that have broken under excessive tightening. Truss rods that are accessible from both ends of the fretboard can usually be replaced without removing the fretboard. In most other cases the fretboard must be removed to install a new truss rod. In any case, forcing glue into position-marker holes will only work for a nonadjustable channel rod or T-bar.

If buzzing persists even after all of the forementioned possibilities have been eliminated, the possibility of resonating dissonance must be considered. This is an unusual condition but by no means rare and may be a flaw uniquely tied to the use of plywood in guitar construction. The principal cause of buzzing in plywood guitars, however, is localized separation of the plies of the wood.

A common focal point of ply separation is the area under the bridge. String tension on the bridge can lift the top veneer to which the bridge is glued. But ply separation can occur almost anywhere and is probably due to the effect of high humidity on a spot where the glue bond is weak. Ply separations can be located by feel or by visual observation during periods of high humidity; a loose ply swollen with moisture will mound up like a blister. Slice open the loose ply with a razor or sharp knife, force glue in through the incision, and clamp.

Resonating dissonance caused by sympathetic vibration is the most elusive source of buzzing or poor sound. It is usually not rooted in any physical construction flaw but is an accidental confluence of certain acoustic factors.

The top, the back, and the sound cavity of a guitar each have a natural resonating pitch, the pitch or frequency level which will generate the strongest

31. *Sounding strings while pressing soundboard to locate sensitive area*

vibrational response. If the pitch of top and back are very close, a coupling effect will swell their amplitude to an unnatural degree. This swollen resonance can be set in motion by playing a chord or note at the same frequency as this resonance. The resultant amplitude competes with the basic resonating pitch of the sound cavity in a kind of acoustic battle for supremacy. All this stress produces an undesirable sympathetic vibration of some sensitive part of the guitar and the end result is dissonance that shows up as buzzing or a poor sound.

When a guitar is made of spruce top and rosewood back—woods of very different density and resonating characteristics—there is little chance of coupling and the resultant acoustic dilemma. In plywood guitars, however (telltale plies can be spotted on the inside edge of the sound hole), there is a flattening out of resonating characteristics with a heightened susceptibility to dissonant buzzing. Guitars of fine tone have been built of plywood but they are the rare exception rather than the rule.

Begin your investigation of resonating dissonance by strumming the strings or individual notes until buzzing or a bad sound can be produced at will. While making this sound, move your right-hand fingertips over the soundboard or have someone else strum while you do this. At some point, finger pressure will result in a marked damping or elimination of the unwanted sound. Circle the area lightly with a china marking crayon and repeat the experiment—induce buzzing, and damp with finger pressure until satisfied that the connection is unmistakable.

Double check inside with mirror and probe to make sure a loose brace is not the real culprit. Cut a small brace of spruce and glue it in place under where the crayon mark was made (Fig. 31). The point is that something must be done to change the way a plate vibrates at a sensitive point. Unfortunately, this whole area of resonating dissonance is one that is not yet clearly understood. Until scientific explanations are forthcoming, it's pretty much every man for himself.

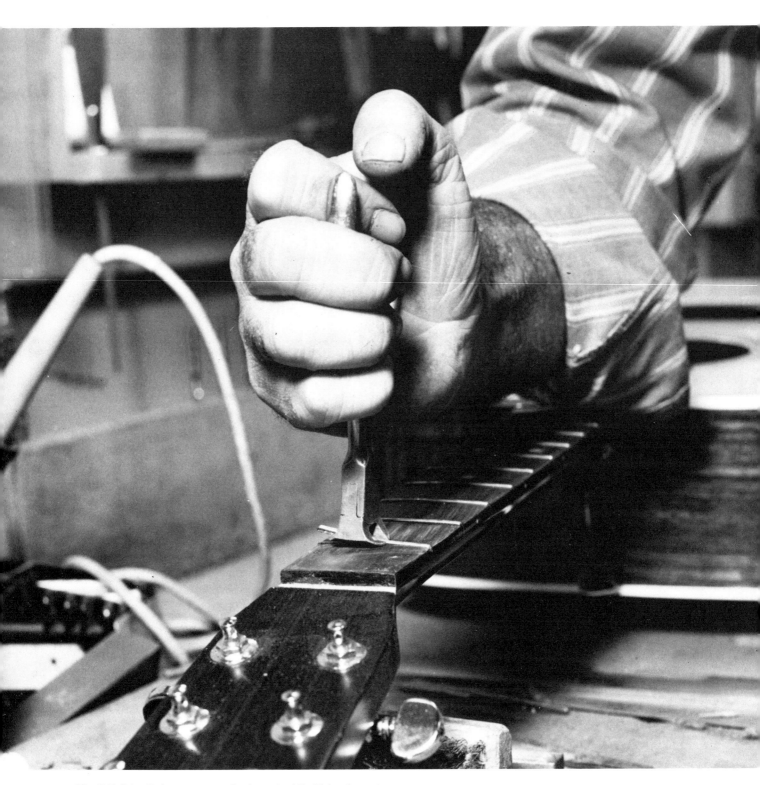

32. "Walking" nippers across fretboard while lifting fret wire

REFRETTING

A wire nipper with a flat nose and wide jaw is the best tool for lifting frets. If you don't have end-cutting nippers, you can make one out of any nipper by simply grinding down the nose until it will bite almost flush. In Figure 38, spring nippers are being used. They make quick work of clipping fret ends and automatically spring open after each bite.

Begin by lifting slightly the corner of the first fret. Move back along this fret about a half inch. Grip the fret loosely with the nippers and "walk" the nose of the nipper along the fretboard, lifting the fret as you go. Do not grip frets in the middle and yank them out. This will arch the fret wire causing the studded tang to pull out at an angle and increase the hazard of fracturing the top edge of the slot.

Frets that have been set in with glue can be loosened by placing a hot pressing iron or soldering iron on the frets before lifting. Do not use a hot iron where the fingerboard is inlaid with ivory or mother-of-pearl (dots excluded) or where the leading edges of the fingerboard are covered with a strip of decorative binding.

Recalcitrant frets can also be removed by first lifting them with a broad chisel. Force the chisel under the fret-wire bead with the bevel of the chisel flat against the fretboard. This will provide enough leverage to lift the frets slightly so that the nipper can finish lifting them out.

Prepare a cardboard or heavy paper pattern to cut out a plastic template. This protective bib is held in place by masking tape to keep sawdust off the soundboard and out of the sound hole. Ebony sawdust has an irritating habit of working its way into a top with a worn or patchy finish.

Preliminary smoothing of the bare fretboard can be done with a small plane angled slightly to give a shearing action and smooth passage over the fret slots. Adjust the plane blade to remove only a slight amount of wood on each pass. Arched fretboards are best smoothed with a long block of wood covered with sandpaper. Frequent checking with a curved template is necessary to make sure the degree of arch remains constant along the entire length of the fretboard. Arching the fretboard is common on many styles of acoustic and plectrum guitars, an innovation apparently borrowed from the viol family and designed to facilitate the fingering of barre chords. The classic guitar fretboard is always dead flat.

While smoothing progresses, the longitudinal surface must be periodically checked with a steel straightedge until the metal edge makes contact with the fretboard all along its length. From this point on the procedure differs depending on whether the guitar is strung with nylon or steel strings. If nylon strings are used, the fretboard is leveled along its entire length.

If the guitar is strung with steel strings, an attempt

34. *Checking arch of fretboard with curved template*

must be made to flex the neck to see if there is any give. If there is any give at all in the neck, expert repairmen prefer to leave a slight degree of back bow in the fretboard, knowing that the high tension of steel strings will pull the neck and fretboard straight. The fretboard is smoothed until it makes contact with a steel straightedge from about the fifth to twelfth (or fourteenth) fret. The rest of the fretboard tapers away from the contact area very, very gradually and to an exceedingly small degree.

When leveling is completed, resaw the old slots to a depth just barely exceeding the depth of the fret-wire tang. A strip of masking tape along the side of the saw blade will serve as a convenient depth guide. Professional repairmen keep a set of fine dovetail saws to cut slots of different thicknesses to accommodate different gauges of fret wire. Dovetail saws can be had in various thicknesses and their thickness can be subtly altered by

filing or hammering off the set of the teeth, if necessary.

It is essential in refretting to use a heavier gauge of fret wire for replacement frets. On ebony fretboards, replacement frets should be the next heavier gauge. Softer rosewood fretboards are refretted with a fret wire two degrees heavier. Fret wire comes in gauges from .018 to .024 and then jumps to .027 thousandths. Half-sizes are available between .018 and .020 thousandths. The thickness of the studded tang changes but the bead size remains the same. A feeler gauge is used to measure the slot size.

After resawing the slots to the proper depth, dress the entrance of each slot with a three-cornered file to remove the corner of each edge. Just one or two light strokes to dull the sharp edges—no more. This will facilitate future lifting of the frets without fracturing or splintering the face of the fretboard.

The use of glue in anchoring frets seems to be a

35. *Lowering top portion of fretboard with scraper blade*

36. *Feeler gauge to determine fret wire gauge*

37. A few firm taps to anchor frets

matter of personal choice. If the tang and slot are properly mated to ensure a really tight fit, then glue is unnecessary. If glue is used—white or hide glue—special care must be taken to make sure all the fret wire shoulders rest solidly on the fretboard. Glue ooze has a deceptive way of filling a narrow crevice, giving the impression that the fret wire is solidly against the wood when in fact it is not.

Cut the frets slightly oversize, about ¼" overhang on each end. Cut all of them beforehand. Run a few drops of water into each slot before installing frets.

Because the frets, when inserted into the many slots of the fretboard, fit tightly and exert a wedging action, their cumulative effect can bow a fretboard. To minimize this possibility, frets are applied in the following order:

From sound hole to one away from body joint
From fifth to first fret
From eleventh (or thirteenth) to sixth fret
Thirteenth (or fifteenth) fret
Twelfth (or fourteenth) fret

The numbers in parentheses are for necks that have

fourteen frets to the body joint.

A neck that is no more than slightly warped can be straightened by making use of the wedging action of frets. Driving in frets with an extra heavy tang will force the fretboard and neck back to horizontal. Use frets of one or two degrees heavier than normal replacement gauge and drive them into the third, fifth, seventh, and ninth fret slots. Check the level of the fretboard to see if any straightening has occurred. If more straightening is needed, continue with fretting of the fourth, sixth, eighth, and tenth frets. Check the level again. If it is straight—and it should be unless the warp was more extreme than this technique can handle—revert to the use of normal fret gauge for the remaining slots.

Position each fret and drive it home with the large polished face of a chasing hammer or any short-handled hammer with a large slightly rounded face. Do not use a fretting hammer for any other purpose. If the face is dented or scarred, these marks will leave their imprint on the fret wire which is relatively soft.

A few firm taps is all that is necessary to seat a fret. Use a hand-held support inside the body and under the

38. Spring-action nipper cutting off fret ends

fretboard when driving in frets near the sound hole. If glue has been used, wipe away all ooze and check each fret to make sure it is in tight with the bottom of each fret bead snug against the fretboard.

39. Filing fret ends flush

Clip off all the ends with a flush cutting nipper and file them flush using a 10″ flat-mill bastard file. File frets on the treble side from the head toward the body, on the bass side from the body toward the head. Always file frets in a manner that tends to push them into the slot rather than pull them out. Apply strips of ¼″ masking tape alongside each fret to protect the fretboard while the frets are being filed.

Gently glide a long carborundum stone or flat file over the tops of the frets. This will level out any remaining unevenness and leave a narrow, flat ridge on top of each fret. This flat ridge is easy to see because of the abrasions left by the stone or file moving over the frets. All filing and rounding of the frets is done with this flat ridge as a point of reference. As the sides of the frets are carefully filed and rounded, the ridge will gradually narrow until it is gone. Each fret end is first beveled and then rounded off.

Two files are used for dressing frets to their final shape—No. 2 and No. 4 extra-fine pillar files that have had all their leading edges ground smooth on a belt sander.

Work slowly and carefully. Practice is necessary to file frets to a uniformly rounded shape with speed and precision. The object of all this patient labor is to ensure a flawless action and smooth passage of a player's fingers over the frets. It is annoying to play a guitar and quickly learn that a protruding fret end snags passing fingers. The player must then get a file and do the job the luthier should have done.

Finish off the frets by polishing them with a worn piece of crocus cloth. Remove the masking-tape strips by peeling them off from each end before lifting them off. If they are yanked away without peeling them loose on both ends, they will take off the finish on the neck.

Guitars, mandolins, and other fretted instruments made before 1933 used solid frets; each fret was a solid bar of metal sized to fit the slot exactly. These frets are not made any more and refretting these instruments requires gluing thin shims of veneer in each slot so that standard frets can be used. This is a tedious procedure and it is sometimes simpler to prepare a new fretboard.

Refretting of guitars that have a decorative strip of binding glued to the long edges of the fretboard requires that each fret be notched before installation. The tang must be cut back so that just the bead overhangs the trim.

Inevitably, in refretting there will be gaps visible along the edge of the fretboard where the slot is deeper than the tang. These holes must be filled by burning-in with a lacquer stick. Sticks come in many colors including black for ebony and are applied with a heated instrument such as a spatula, knife, or fine soldering tip.

The lacquer stick is held near the hole to be filled and the heated knife is held against the stick until a small portion is melted and transferred to the hole. This is the same burning-in technique furniture finishers use for filling minor dents and scratches in both finished and unfinished wood. For the purpose of filling the holes under fret ends, a small soldering iron works well. After the holes are filled and dry, sand smooth.

The resurfacing of ebony fretboards sometimes exposes streaks or veinings of light gray. If these markings are unobtrusive they will eventually disappear, darkened by the oil and perspiration of the player's hand. If they are prominent they can be dyed black with a stain (*Ebonholzbeize*) sold by guitar and violin supply houses. Apply with a cotton swab, allow to penetrate, and then wipe clean.

Finish the fretboard with a light coat of refined linseed oil rubbed to a soft sheen with a clean rag.

40. *Filing down solid fret replacements*

41. Rounding off corners of fret ends

42. Filling gaps under frets with lacquer stick and soldering iron

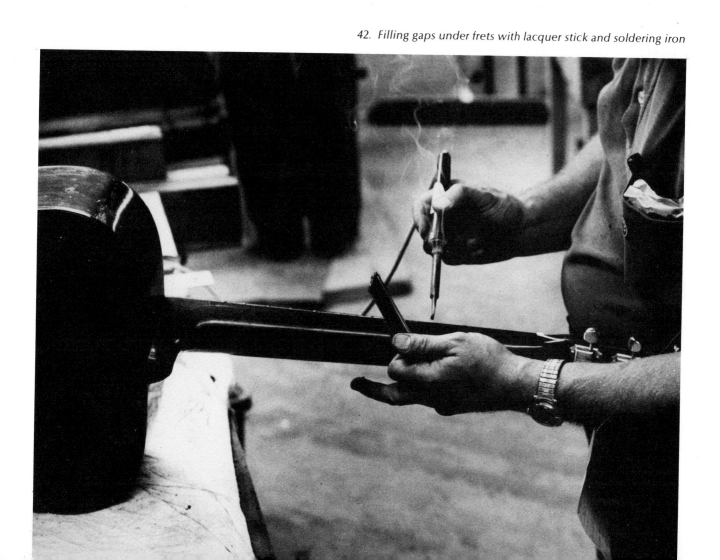

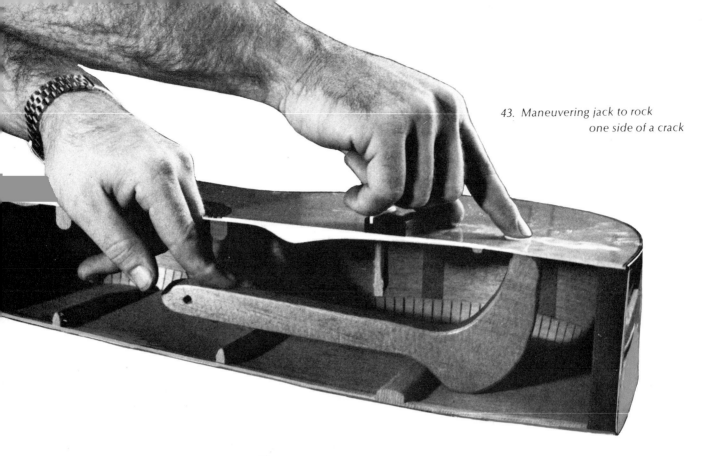

CRACKS

Hairline cracks occur as a result of sudden, severe drying out of wood that has been swollen with moisture; weak points in the grain structure grow progressively weaker as drying continues until hairline fissures appear. Over a long period of time the wood surrounding hairline cracks will shrink until the cracks become open separations in the wood. Distinct separations are much harder to repair than hairline cracks, so early attention to cracks is advised.

Begin by preparing a small wooden stud (Fig. 46), a beveled, diamond-shaped piece of wood that will be glued along the underside of the crack after the crack has been glued together. For a soundboard crack, cut the diamond from a leftover piece of spruce. Cracks in rosewood should be studded with diamonds made of rosewood. If the stud has to be applied through the sound hole, it must be beveled beforehand. Bevel the four edges with a chisel and sand smooth.

Clean the area around the crack with a damp cloth. It is not necessary to disturb the finish to repair a hairline crack but the finish should be cleansed of dirt. Position mirror and work lamp inside the guitar where the underside of the crack can be observed. Using an eye-dropper deposit one or two drops of water on the crack. Rub the water into the crack until signs of wetness appear on the underside of the crack. Position a wooden jack alongside the crack (Fig. 43) on the inside of the guitar. The jack is essentially for use where fingers cannot reach the underside of the crack. Rub white glue into the crack and gently rock the jack so that one side of the crack moves up and down, forcing glue into every part of the crack.

Wipe away glue ooze with a damp cloth. Remove the jack and clamp with a deep-throat clamp using two cauls made of plexiglass. Clear plastic cauls give a view of the crack under pressure and also will not bond to polyvinyl glue. The problem of positioning the inside caul can be handled by temporarily securing it in place with masking tape. Not much clamping pressure is needed, since the main purpose of clamping is to ensure that both edges of the crack glue in perfect alignment.

When dry, sand smooth the inner surface of the crack, apply white glue to the stud and position it with the aid of light and mirror. One way of doing this for a soundboard crack is by taping in place a piece of thin

44. *Best glue applicator—fingers*

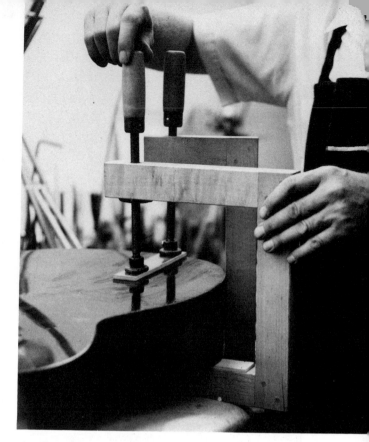

45. *Clamping with plexiglas caul to align crack edges while gluing*

cardboard that has an oversize diamond shape cut out of it. Position the cutout under the crack and use it as a guide for accurately placing the stud. Rub the stud back and forth a few times until the glue starts to set and take hold. Studs applied with this kind of rubbed fit need not be clamped.

For maximum benefit, the stud grain must run crosswise to the grain of the cracked wood. One stud will suffice for a crack less than three inches long. Where several studs are used, they should be kept small and neat to minimize any possible effect on tone. Cracks themselves, even long ones, seem to have little effect on tone, and studding also appears to have no appreciable effect on tone.

46. *Neat, small studding is possible with back off; larger studs are necessary when working through sound hole*

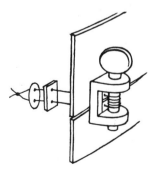

Device for studding inaccessible side crack. Lead two fine wires through a tiny hole drilled above and below crack. Gather wires at soundhole and lead through stud, metal disc, and knot. Apply glue and draw up tight.

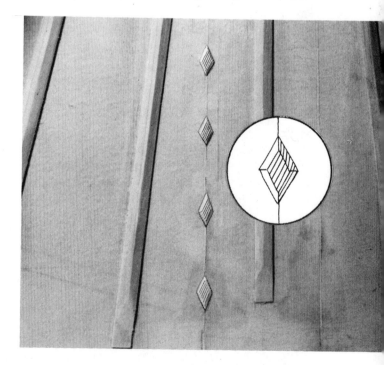

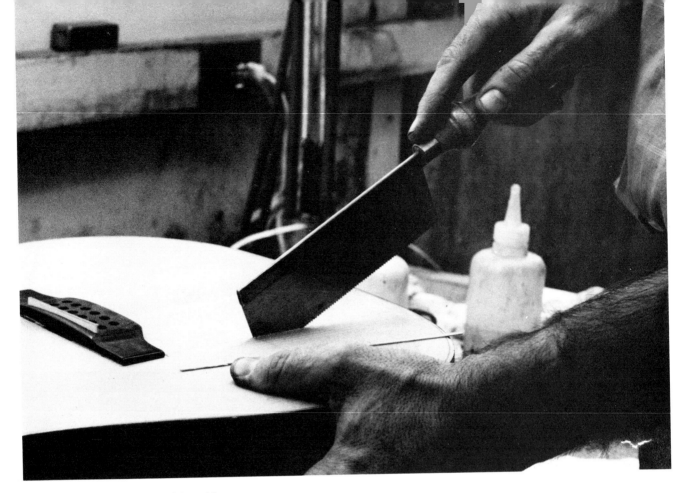

47. Separated crack being widened by saw

48. Sawing off narrow splint

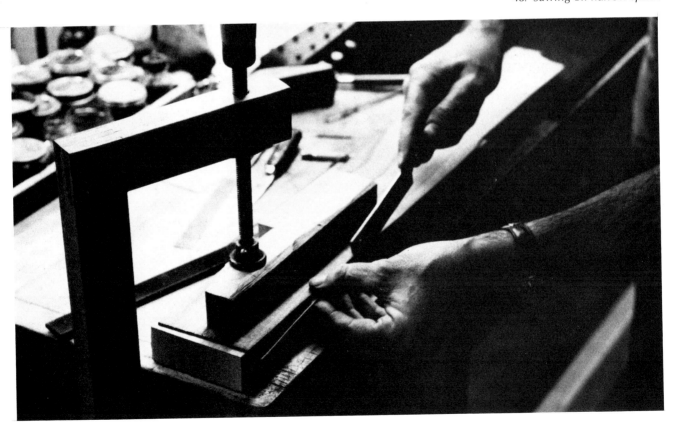

SEPARATED CRACKS

When the wood surrounding older cracks has shrunk and the crack becomes an actual opening, it must be repaired by piecing-in a new piece of wood—a splint. Separated cracks should never be repaired by gluing with a clamp across the body to close the crack. Wood that has-cracked and gradually adapted to a new conformation has a memory. It cannot be pressured into a new conformation with glue and clamps. As soon as the pressure is removed the wood memory will assert itself, and slowly, inexorably, the wood will return to the conformation decreed by a long process of cellular and molecular adaptation. In guitar-making, where sides are bent into a complex curve, wood memory is a factor of serious account. An increase in moisture content will tend to straighten a curve; a decrease will cause a curve to become sharper. This principle also applies in the formation of separated cracks. Swollen with moisture, the crack remains closed. When drying occurs, the

49. Filing sides of splint to slight wedge-shape

50. Tapered crack knife used to make
    crack parallel and wedge-shaped

51. Trying the splint for fit

crack opens. The drying phase is the more crucial determinant in long-term wood adaptation.

Begin by making sure whether the crack has in fact separated by placing the work light inside the guitar and darkening the room. Light through the crack means a separation.

The first step in repairing a separated crack involves enlarging the separation so that it can be pieced with a splint. This enlargement is extended beyond the actual length of the crack to the nearest logical terminus. The shaded areas in Figure 56 show the manner of gapping differently located cracks. Cracks that occur in the soundboard between the rosette and bridge are opened up to the edge of the rosette and terminated under the bridge (the bridge must be removed). If the crack runs down below the bridge, the gap is carried down to the bottom binding.

Using a fine dovetail saw, saw open the crack for its entire length, taking care not to saw through any braces or struts. The opening must then be finished with a crack knife, a wedge-shaped, tapered knife that is repeatedly drawn down the length of the crack until the crack takes the tapered shape of the knife. The knife being used in Figure 50 was ground from a flat file to the shape diagramed next to it. The slightly tapered sides of the crack will keep the splint from falling through, and since the splint is also tapered, a wedging action results that ensures a tight fit. The trick in using the knife is to keep it at the same level for its entire traverse along the crack. The sides of the finished gap should be exactly parallel over the entire length of the gap. The width of the gap should be the same width as the annular division—the space between two dark lines in the grain—for splinting a crack in a soundboard. For other cracks, the width of the gap should be no less than $^3/_{64}$", the smallest practical dimension for fashioning a splint.

For the splint, select a wood scrap of matching color, grain, and appearance, and thicker than the wood to be splinted. If the splint is going to be pieced into a top where the finish is not going to be removed,

52. White glue applied to length of crack

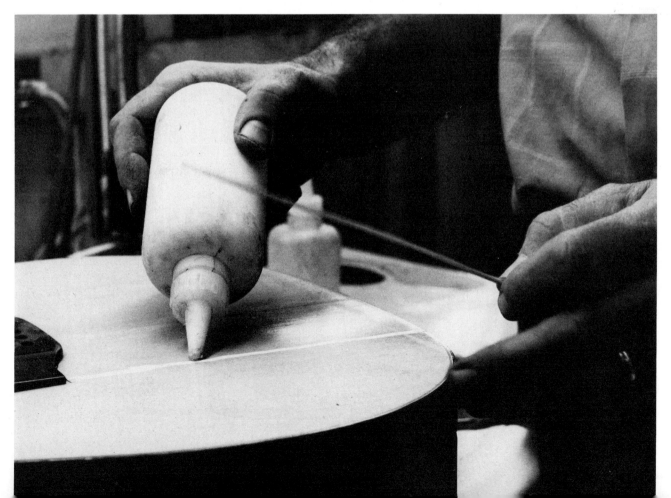

53. Rubbing glue with finger to ensure thorough dispersion through crack

54. Pressing in splint with smooth face of hammer

the scrap to be used must be tested. Daub a spot of lacquer on the scrap outside the area you will use for the splint. Compare the dried spot with the top. Wood color is deceptive and what may look like one color in a raw, sanded condition may turn out after finishing to be a much different shade than originally anticipated. Test-lacquering of a small piece of wood increases the likelihood of a close color match.

Having chosen a suitable splint material, clamp it in the manner shown in Figure 48. Shave the edge with a small block plane angled slightly to produce a slight bevel. Saw off the splint so that it is slightly larger than the gap. Lay the splint on its beveled side and bevel the other side with a wide, flat bastard file.

It is essential when working with the splint to keep it free of oily perspiration. If your hands have a tendency to perspire, use tweezers or lightweight cotton gloves when handling the splint.

After beveling both sides, try the splint for fit. Firmly press it into the gap and mark the cut-off place on both ends. Keep trying and filing the splint until it fits. When firmly pressed into the gap, a small part of the splint should still protrude above the surface of the top. Check with the work light inside the guitar to make sure there is no light seepage indicating irregularity in the fit of the splint. When the splint fits with no light seepage, lay a piece of paper or cloth inside the guitar under the splint to catch glue drippings.

Apply white glue or hot, clear animal glue to both splint and gap. Use a small artist's brush and work fast. This operation must be accomplished quickly so that the splint can be inserted before the water in the glue starts to swell the wood. Insert one hand into the guitar and put your fingers under the gap. Use the chasing hammer to tap home the splint. Run the hammer face over the splint, wedging it home with firm pressure. Feel with your fingers along the bottom edge of the crack to make sure that the splint finishes flush or even protrudes slightly.

When the splint is dry, file or plane off the excess wood and scrape the inside to remove glue beads and excess wood. Sand both sides smooth.

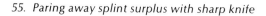

55. Paring away splint surplus with sharp knife

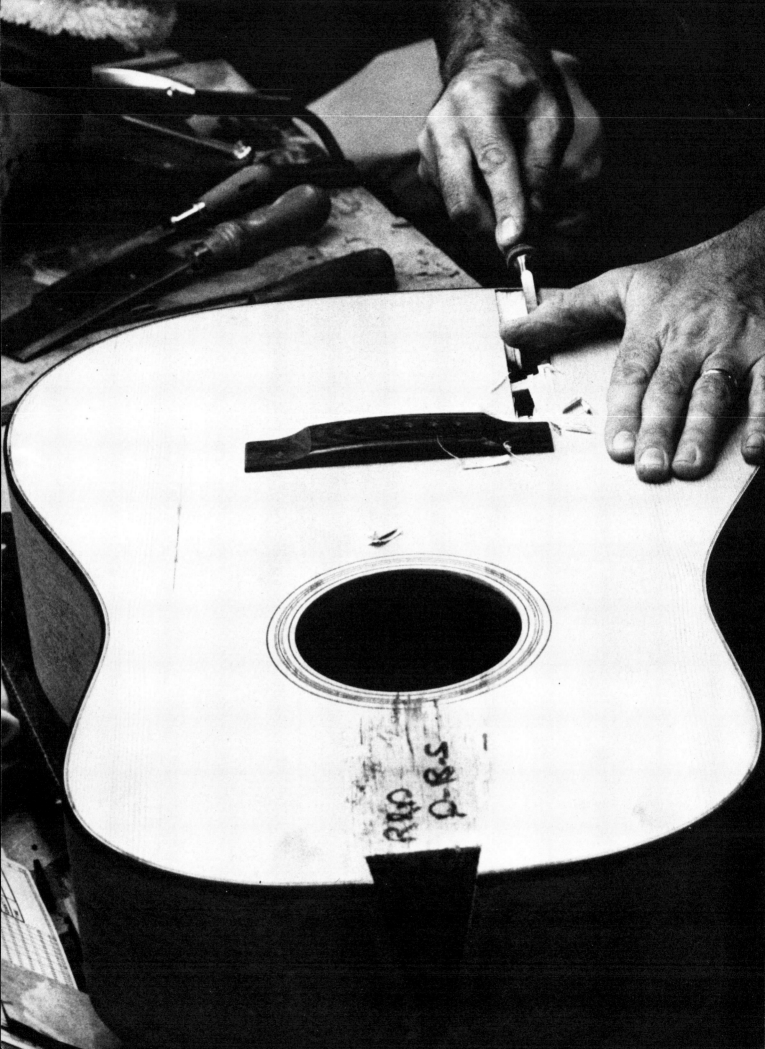

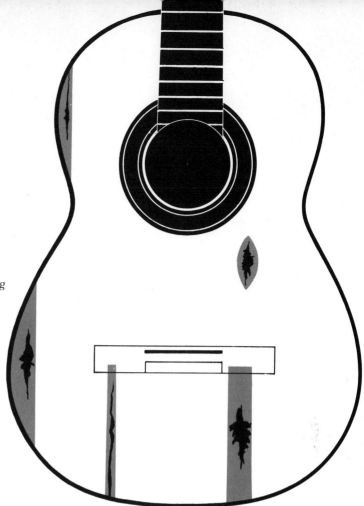

56. Gray areas show patching or splinting shapes for different locations. Floating patches are usually reserved for darker rosewood sides and backs.

FRACTURES

Guitars that have serious holes or fractures are the most challenging and difficult to repair. Great patience and a practiced eye are needed in order to make repairs that do not make it obvious that the instrument has been patched.

The location of the fracture determines the size and shape of the patch to be pieced-in. Figure 56 shows the kinds of patches used for different locations. Neatness and simplicity are the ruling principles. The poorest kind of patch is a square one whose ends terminate at right angles to the grain leaving a glue line that runs crossgrain. Such a patch makes concealment of the repair impossible; just the difference in reflective quality of the patch and the wood at the points where they meet at a crossgrain division would advertise the presence of the patch. For this reason, square-ended patches are never used. Patches situated in an open, unbounded area—floating patches—are always foot-ball-shaped, pointed ovals. They offer the best chance of concealment.

Grain, color, and reflective quality are all critical factors in selecting a patch. An invisible piecing-in will only result from the careful matching of the new piece to the wood surrounding the fracture. And to match them properly it is necessary to remove the finish from that face of the guitar where the fracture lies. Varnish and other finishes so alter the visual character of wood that matching with an unfinished patch is a risky business. Masking tape and paper can be used to isolate top, sides, or back while the finish is removed from the affected portion. Use a nonwaxy, cream-type remover that will soften the finish enough to permit easy removal with a broad scraper or putty knife. When the finish is removed down to the bare wood, cleanse the surface with a rag moistened with turpentine. Make sure that every trace of the remover is gone. If the

57. Cleaning out fracture with chisel

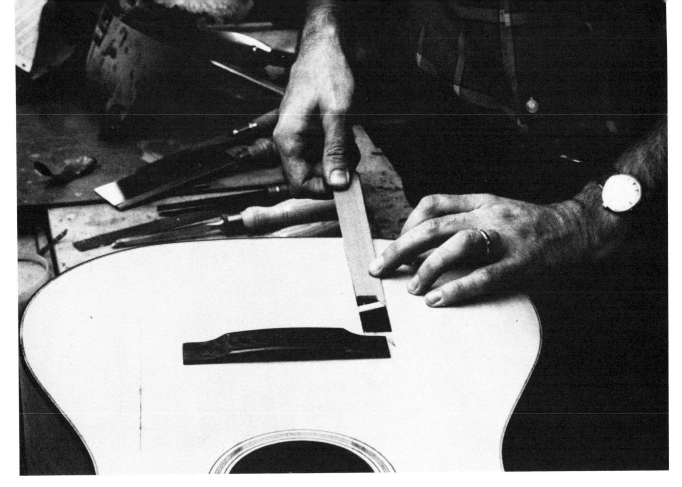

58. *Trying slightly tapered wide splint for fit*

59. *With splint wedged tightly in place, overhang is marked for cutting*

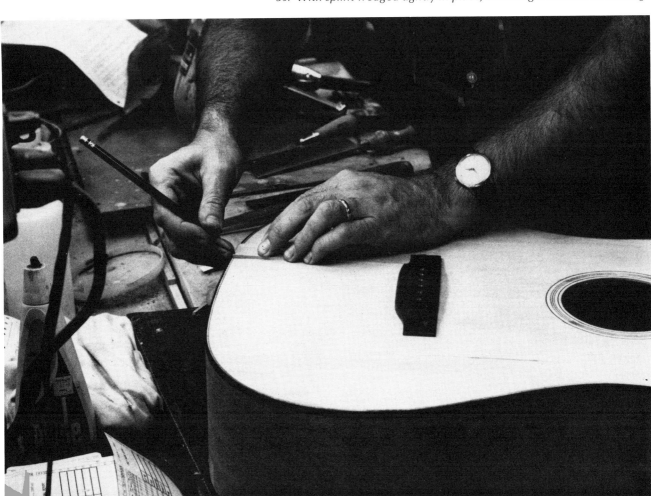

60. Before and after splinting

fracture is a gaping hole, seal it off with masking tape applied to the inside of the guitar, under the hole. This will keep the remover and dissolved finish from dripping into the interior of the guitar.

When a patch is chosen, place it over the fracture. Reverse its position to gauge its reflective quality from opposite directions. Use the direction that appears most in harmony with the surrounding wood.

Soundboard fractures that have at least one end against the edge binding can be repaired with a broad, tapered splint that will wedge into final position. Floating patches must be seated in an opening whose edges are slightly beveled to keep the patch from falling through. Where the wedging principle can be used, beveling is unnecessary.

When the exact shape of the repair has been decided, cut a pattern out of a thin piece of cardboard. Trace this pattern in place over the fracture to be patched. The fracture is always cut to the patching

shape before the patch is made. Fractures can be cut to size with a sharp knife (Fig. 62) or a piece of jigsaw blade held in a vise action handle sold for this purpose. Cut well inside the penciled outline, leaving the final shaping of the beveled opening to be done with a half-round file.

Fractures that run lengthwise with the grain are cut to the patch or splint size with a sharp knife. Cut through with light, repeated incisions rather than one powerful stroke that might crack the wood. After cutting a deep incision around the fracture, clean out the waste wood with a chisel. Be careful in using the knife and chisel that you do not cut into interior struts and braces. If you are uncertain about the position of these interior parts, insert the work light into the guitar and darken the room. Trace onto the top of the guitar the outline of the braces that cross the patching area. This interior lighting technique will not work with opaque wood such as rosewood.

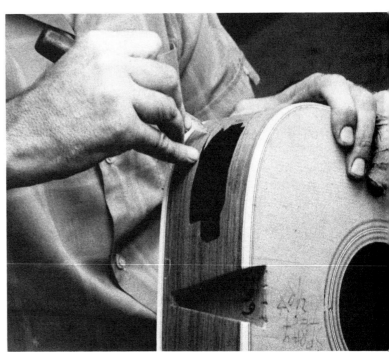

62. Cutting out patch area with sharp knife

61. Cardboard template for outlining a floating side patch

63. Filing smooth finished patch

64. Bending moistened wood for side replacement

65. Gluing in kerfed lining with clothespin clamps

66. Side patch ready for gluing

67. Edges of patch are beveled to prevent patch from falling through

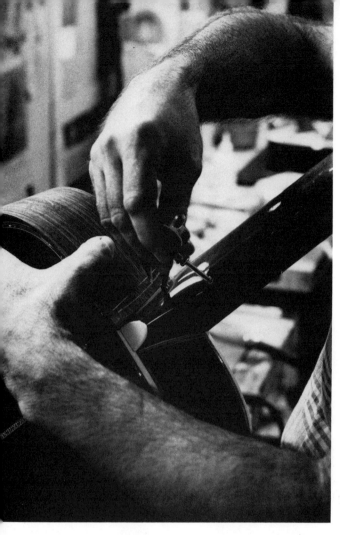

68. *Transferring heel contour to top end of side patch with dividers*

69. *Elbow clamp to hold side patch in place while gluing*

For wedge splints or patches that have one edge against the edge binding, leave enough wood to overhang this edge. Use the cardboard pattern to cut out the patch. Proceed slowly, fitting and refitting the patch until it gradually acquires the precise shape needed for a tight fit. There is no fast way of doing this. It is always a slow, painstaking process needing a critical eye and large amounts of ungrudging patience.

After final fitting of a wedge splint has been achieved and the overhang has been neatly amputated to fit snugly against the binding, it is time to glue. Apply white glue to all gluing edges (remember the cloth inside the box to catch drips) and wedge the splint into place. After the joint is dry, plane the splint flush.

When a football-type patch is ready for gluing it should be checked with mirror and work light to make sure there are no gaps. Apply glue to gluing edges and press the patch into place. Wipe away all glue ooze and

place plastic cauls cut larger than the patch area above and below the patch and clamp. In Figure 69 a round elbow clamp is used to make sure the patch won't spring out of place. After this side patch was glued in, a wide strip of brown muslin was glued to the underside of the patch area as an added reinforcement. First, the inside surface was smoothed with sandpaper to unite the patch and adjacent wood in an unbroken, smooth surface. The muslin strip was cut to cover an area larger than the patch. It was saturated with white glue and carefully placed in position over the patch area. A long, stiff wire with a rubber ball on the end of it was run over the muslin to smooth out wrinkles (Fig. 72). This is trickier than it sounds and requires some practice. When the muslin dries it shrinks tight against the wood making an excellent reinforcement for the patch. A good substitute is a wide strip of Mystic tape. It is self-sticking and will serve almost as well.

70. Trimming out muslin for patch reinforcement

71. Spreading white glue on muslin

60

72. *Muslin positioned and being smoothed by rubber ball on the end of a slender rod*

73. Replacement for full side

74. Side cleaned and ready for replacement

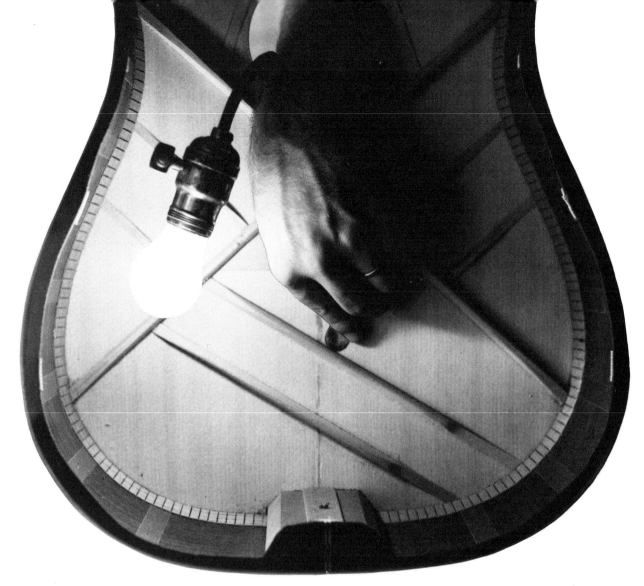

75. *Probing brace with work light inside and mirror handy*

LOOSE BRACES

One's forearm girth permitting, it is possible to make many repairs working through the sound hole of the guitar. Loose braces, a common source of buzzing, can be located with a probing spatula and then glued tight. Various kinds of body cracks and fractures can also be repaired without removing the affected members—top, back, and sides—by using the sound hole for access to the interior.

Practice with the trouble light and mirror will quickly bring facility in checking the interior. Figure 75 shows a probe being run along the glue joint of a brace,

probing for the smallest sign of separation. A sudden penetration of the probe into a separated joint can immediately be felt even though the probing is conducted blind.

A careful mirror inspection through the sound hole should include the following points of interest:

> *Both sides of all braces and struts*
> *Linings where they glue to sides and top*
> *Reinforcing plate under the bridge*
> *Possible cracks in soundboard alongside*
> *the fretboard*

When a loose brace has been located, check with work light and mirror to see the length of the separation. When this has been carefully noted, remove the work light and mirror. Hold the guitar in your lap and with forearm through the sound hole, find out whether

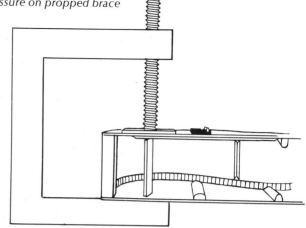

you can comfortably reach the separation with your fingers. If your fingers can reach this spot, then situate the guitar so that gluing can be accomplished with the aid of gravity. If the loose brace is one of the longitudinal tone braces glued to the soundboard, turn the guitar face down in your lap or as nearly so as possible while still permitting through-the-sound-hole maneuvering. Place a clean rag inside the guitar, close to the brace to be glued. This will facilitate cleaning up drips which are almost impossible to avoid.

Apply white glue with a finger or—if the separation is hard to reach—with a spatula, bent if necessary to permit sliding the glue into the separation. Wipe clean immediately with a slightly dampened cloth, being sure to remove all excess glue from surrounding areas. Check with the mirror to make sure the glue has penetrated all parts of the separation.

Gently wedge a wooden prop (Fig. 76) between the separated brace and the back, positioned exactly under the freshly glued section. Secure a large box clamp around the body so that clamping pressure is applied in a vertical line over the hidden prop. Use good-sized protective cauls to help spread the clamping pressure in case your clamp is not in line with the prop (Fig. 77). Prepare props beforehand and it is a good idea to stockpile an assortment in graduated sizes. The wedging action should be slight, just enough to ensure that the prop won't fall out, and the clamping pressure should be firm but not excessive. An oversized prop can crack the top or back.

Leave under pressure for several hours. When dry remove the clamp and prop and check with the mirror to see if the separation is glued tight. Scrape away glue beads that may have oozed out after clamping and remove any trace of glue that may have dried on adjacent areas.

77. Clamping with large caul over propped area

REMOVING TOP and BACK

The most serious kind of damage such as a massive fracture or a hopeless distortion of the top or back will necessitate their removal and replacement. It does not really matter if they are damaged in the process of removing them, but for purposes of duplication it is best to remove them in relatively intact condition. It makes it easier to orient new struts and braces in their correct position.

Begin removal of a top by making a simple diagram noting the measurements of the distance from nut to saddle and the exact placement of the sound hole. Draw a center line down the face of the fretboard with a white china marking crayon. This line will help align the fretboard when it is reassembled.

Remove the bridge using the procedure described on page 75. Lift the fret wire at the juncture of neck and body and saw down through this fret slot until the fretboard is severed. Lift the soundboard portion of the fretboard with a broad spatula, heat lamp, and water, if necessary. This piece is salvaged to glue back again on the new soundboard.

When the fretboard section is off, force a small, fine probe into the glue joint between the edge binding and the sides. Work the probe along the entire glue joint. Use the probe to free the binding from the edge of the soundboard and strip it carefully away from the guitar.

A saber saw will quickly remove the major portion of the top. Saw around the entire perimeter of the guitar about 1" from the edge. Be sure to skirt the top

79. Removing top quickly with saber saw

80. Carefully checking fit of top before gluing

81. Bookbinder's screw press is used for clamping top and back; tapered wedges are inserted to apply more pressure along glue joint

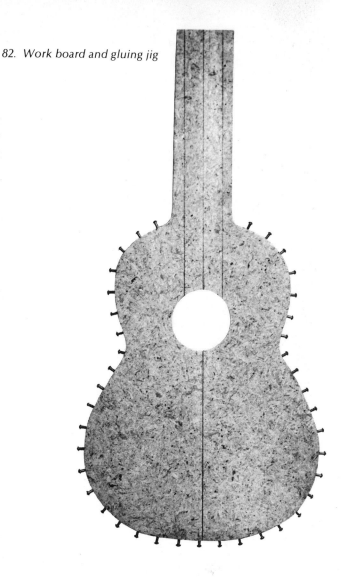

and bottom blocks with the saw.

Use a large probe or chisel to free all the sound-board fragments still glued to the sides. Avoid splintering or loosening the kerfed lining to which the top must glue. All broken sections will have to be replaced before gluing on a new top.

Clean off the old glue from the top of the lining, from the sides and from both blocks. When cleaning off the top of the dovetail block beware of removing wood. If the top of this block is lowered it will be necessary to use a thicker soundboard to ensure that the reassembled fingerboard will line up in the same plane. Scrape clean the open sections in the lining where the strut ends will glue to the sides.

The old rosette can be salvaged by nailing the old top face down on a board and routing away the wood until the rosette is almost reached. Work a sharp knife around the edge of the rosette until it is freed. But unless the rosette is of some special value, it is simpler to install a new one.

The back is removed in the same way. Both plates can be removed intact by using a heated spatula to free the plates after the bindings are removed.

It is important to note that removing either top or back weakens the structure of the guitar and may alter the shape of the sides. It is always best to do this work with the guitar held in a form. A spreader clamp is useful for immobilizing the sides while working on them (Fig. 78).

For gluing plates back onto the guitar, professional repairmen use a press (Fig. 81). After hide glue has been applied to the linings and top edge of the sides, the plate is put in place and the guitar body is placed in the press. Pressure is applied and tapered wedges are jammed in around the edges to apply more pressure to the glue joint.

A simple gluing jig can be made out of a ¾" × 16" × 34" piece of pressed wood. Jigsaw the shape to the pattern (Fig. 82) and sand the outline smooth. Insert 1" round-head rustproof screws all around the perimeter of the form spaced 1½" apart. Screw them in until the thread is buried and only the smooth shank is left. Rubber bands are looped around these screws and laced back and forth across the body of the guitar to exert pressure while the top or back is glued on. A one-pound box ⅝" × 7" rubber bands will provide an adequate supply for lacing.

83. Rubber bands apply pressure to freshly glued top

84. *Electric router with router bit in place*

85. *Adjustable purfling cutter for guitars*

SEAM SEPARATION, BINDINGS

Where seams have separated along the bound edges of top or back, they should be repaired as soon as the separation occurs. Separations left too long tend to drift further apart and become more difficult to repair.

Forcing two edges together with a clamp is always a risky business. If moderate hand pressure cannot bring the parted joint into easy conjunction, then other methods must be employed.

A narrow separation of the binding plies can be filled by burning-in with a lacquer stick of the right color. If a separation occurs between the bindings and the top or back, a careful inspection must be made to find out if the plate has broken its glue joint with the lining inside. Seam separations of this kind, even narrow ones, cannot be repaired by burning-in with a lacquer stick. It is better to splint the separation with a narrow piece of wood tapered on both ends. More serious separations can be handled as a patching job.

Advanced separations can sometimes be corrected by installing a wider binding. This is a major task and in the case of a top involves removing the fretboard. And unless there is sufficient lining to support the additional binding width, this method cannot be used.

To remove the bindings, carefully scrape away the finish over the glue joint along the side of the binding. Use a short, thin clock-spring probe to separate this glue joint. The penetration of the probe must be carefully controlled to avoid separating the top or back from the lining. When the glue joint has been parted along the whole side of the binding, the binding can easily be separated from its top joint and removed. This operation plus the widening of the binding ledge can be quickly accomplished with a routing machine and carbide-tipped cutting bit (Fig. 84). A ball bearing serves as a pilot. The same job can be done with a hand purfling cutter adjusted to the proper cutting width. If a

86. *Half the binding bound in place*

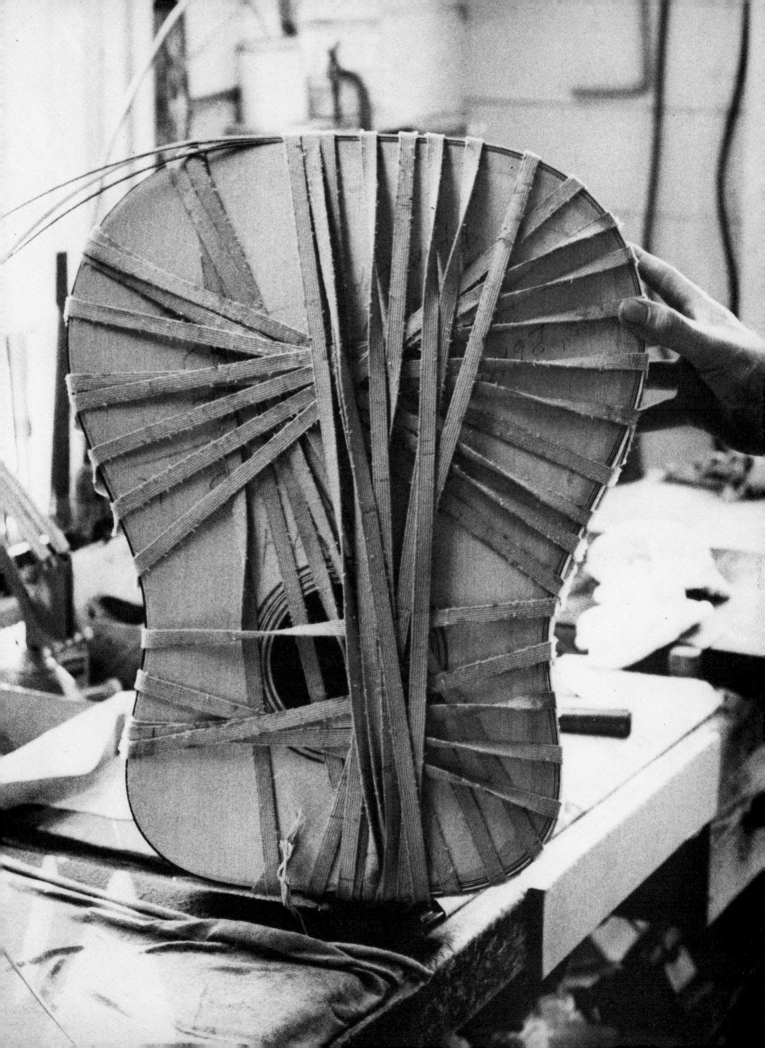

hand cutter is used the cut is made before the bindings are removed.

Bindings are available in either plastic or wood and are glued and bound in place simultaneously. Figures 89-91 illustrate the manner of binding a guitar with 1″ upholsterer's canvas tape. Practice this binding pattern before undertaking the actual job. Firm pressure must be kept on the tape while glue is quickly applied to the different plies of the binding. As the plies are bent into place, excess glue is wiped away with a damp cloth and the tape is wrapped in a sequence that ensures uniform pressure throughout. Half the binding is laid on and glued at one time. When the first half is dry, the second half is bound.

White glue will work well with wood bindings but not with plastic bindings. Duco cement is a better choice for most of the plastic bindings being used by manufacturers today.

It is important to remember that bindings seal off the end grain of top and back. Once the end grain is exposed, atmospheric moisture is absorbed at an accelerated rate and the possibility of wood distortion greatly increases. In seriously advanced cases of neglect it is sometimes necessary to replace a top or back.

89. Cleaning off excess cement

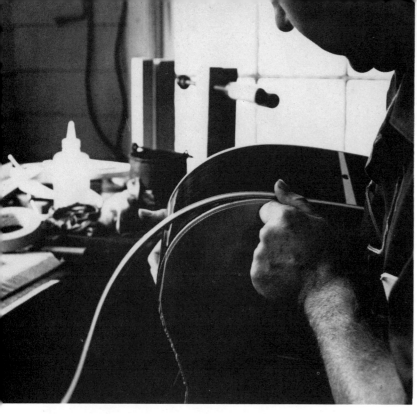

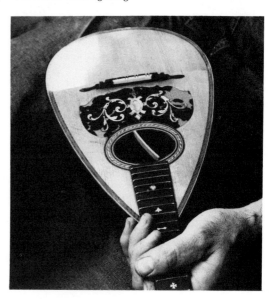

88. Wooden prop used to wedge loose trim while gluing

87. Separating old binding with small probe

90. Tape is wound on tight while bindings are held in place

91. Half the binding is taped in place at one time

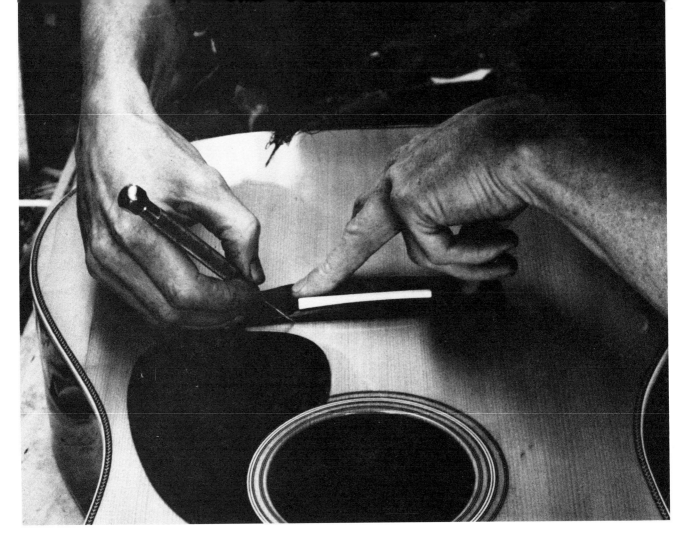

92. *Scribing outline of bridge position*

BRIDGE, BELLYING of TOP

93. *Straightedge shows bellying of bridge area*

The bridge is a vital link in the transmission of string vibrations to the soundboard. It is also the focal point of all string tension and sometimes—during humid, hot conditions particularly—the bridge will come loose.

Cracks in bridges are confined mainly to pin bridges and occur through the misguided application of force—a hammer usually—to wedge in a pin more securely. If the string is in the tapered pin-hole groove and the ball end is properly lodged against the reinforcing plate under the bridge, the string will stay there with the pin inserted with just moderate hand pressure. Besides the risk of cracking the bridge, continually forcing in the pin will eventually enlarge the hole to the point where the wedging action is lost. When this happens, a new, thicker set of pins will have to be fitted to the enlarged holes.

94. *Cracking off bridge with wide chisel*

A cracked bridge must be removed in order to repair it. If the crack is minor, gluing and clamping are all that need be done. Seriously cracked bridges must be replaced.

String tension over a long period of time can lift the bridge, along with the soundboard area that surrounds it, into a mounded belly. This is primarily a problem of steel-string guitars and is a sign that the soundboard itself or the internal bracing of the soundboard was not strong enough to cope with the string pull on the bridge. A certain amount of top lift is normal and has no effect on the playability of the guitar.

Tops differ in density, grain, and flexibility and some are inherently weaker than others. Such tops will belly more easily, especially when subjected to excessive string tension for protracted periods of time.

Another cause of bellying is loose bracing.

The combination of weak top and excessive tension can belly a top to the point where the bridge is tilted out of its horizontal plane; the back end of the bridge pulls the soundboard up into a pronounced hump and the front edge depresses the portion of the soundboard that lies between bridge and sound hole.

If bellying is far enough advanced it will affect the action. Restoring the action will necessitate eliminating the belly so that the bridge will be returned to its proper position. To do this, you must remove the bridge and—on steel-string guitars—the reinforcing plate glued under the bridge area. On nylon-string guitars where a weak or thin top has resulted in twisting of the bridge and serious bellying, a new top is the best solution.

Begin by scribing a fine line around the edge of the

73

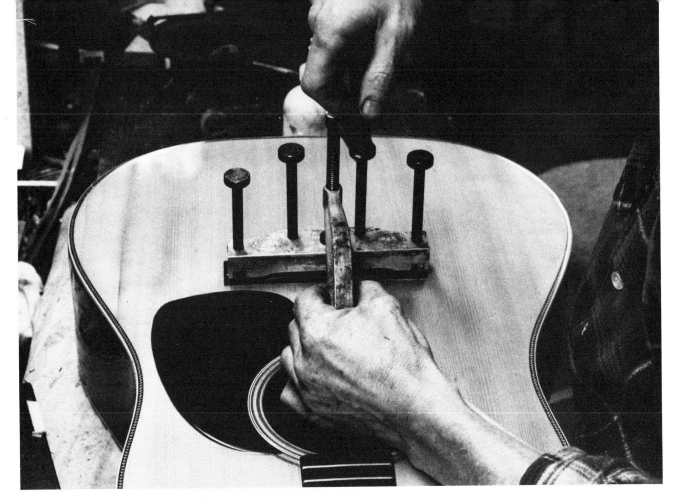

95. *Aluminum clamping jig for bridge*

96. *Clamping arrangement for reinforcing plate*

bridge to mark its exact position. Place a chisel or wide spatula against the glue line of a corner of the bridge and tap it with a mallet. Crack the glue line of all four corners of the bridge before trying to lift the long edges of the bridge. This will considerably lessen the hazard of cracking the top or the finish when lifting the bridge.

Move the chisel to the long edges of the bridge and continue tapping. When it begins to lift on the long edges, watch for uneven resistance. Lift the bridge from the side that offers the least resistance. Wood fibers loosened from the soundboard and stuck to the bottom of the bridge will make lifting against the grain more difficult. Lifting with the grain will also prevent further splintering. As a rule, bridges come off easily. Unusually stubborn cases can be helped by employing a heat lamp. Protect the adjacent wood with an asbestos mask and use probes to work through the softened glue.

Working with a curved probe, reach inside the guitar and crack the glue line along the leading edges of the reinforcing plate. Taking care not to dig into the top, gradually work the probe deeper and deeper until the reinforcing plate comes loose. Check with mirror and clear the area of all wood fragments and old glue.

Reinforcing plates are hardwood—rosewood or maple usually—and are cut so the grain runs crossgrain to the grain of the top. Prepare a new plate following the outline of the old one but with an increased depth (Fig. 97). The increase in the depth of the plate will depend on how serious the belly is. Enough gluing area must be provided to flatten the belly and ensure against its future recurrence. At the same time do not use an unnecessarily large plate, since any additional wood glued to the soundboard can have a damping effect on sound.

Position a ³⁄₄″ × 4″ × 8″ wooden caul over the bridge area and apply white glue to the new plate. Press the plate into place and clamp as shown in Figure 96. The large box clamps are used to force down the soundboard and plate into a slightly reverse curve. Leave under pressure for several days. When clamps and caul are removed, the soundboard should spring back flat.

Sand smooth the bottom of the bridge by sliding it over a piece of sandpaper taped to a flat surface. Using a chisel or small scraper, scrape clean the area within

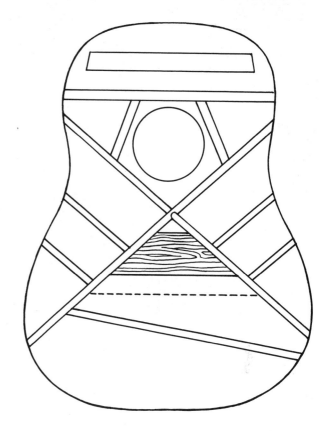

97. Dotted line shows enlarged depth of reinforcing plate replacement.

the scribed outline of the bridge. All traces of old glue must be removed and both gluing surfaces should be perfectly smooth. In laboratory tests conducted by the U.S. Department of Agriculture it was found that no benefit was gained by intentional roughening of gluing surfaces.

For efficient clamping of a bridge while gluing, it is useful to have a fitted inside caul, one with grooves to accommodate the braces that cross beneath the bridge area. Without a fitted caul made of metal or hardwood, the clamps will have to be carefully positioned to avoid the braces.

White glue is perfectly adequate for gluing a bridge. Do not use epoxy glues for this purpose. It is far better for the bridge to fly off because of excessive tension than to have the whole top lift away because the bridge has been permanently bonded to the top.

Apply deep-throat clamps and clean away squeezed-out glue with a damp cloth. Leave under pressure overnight.

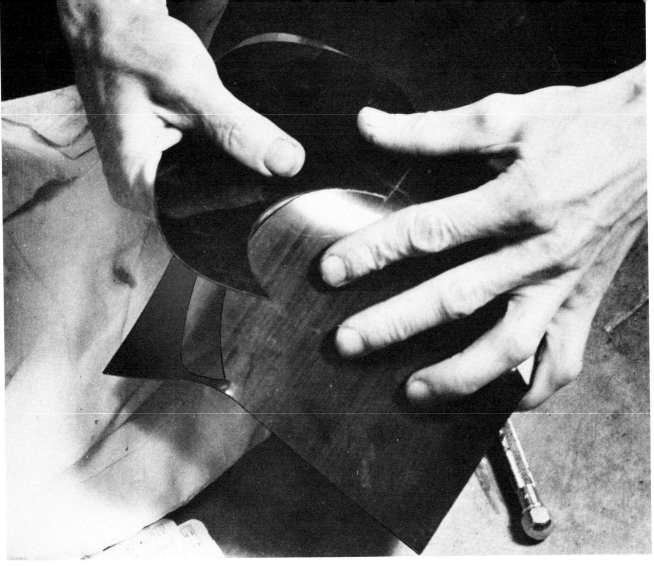

98. Breaking out pick guard after inscribing shape with sharp scriber

PICK GUARDS

Pick guards that are glued to the soundboard are usually made of flexible cellulose acetate material. They are cut in a great variety of shapes and sizes and glued in place before the guitar is lacquered. Adhesion is not accomplished with glue but with a special solvent solution that softens the plastic until it will adhere to wood. The same solution is used to remove the pick guard and cleanse the wood underneath. Extreme caution is necessary in handling the solvent because it will mar a lacquer finish.

The Flexcraft Company (see List of Suppliers, page 95) manufactures a cellulose acetate solvent called No. 337. A pick guard can be removed by lifting a corner of the guard and carefully applying some of the solvent with a small oil can or eye-dropper. As the plastic softens, continue to lift the guard and keep applying the solvent until the guard comes off. Cleanse the area with a cloth dipped in the solvent.

Cut a cardboard template of the new guard's shape. If the old guard is being replaced with the same shape, use the old guard as a template. Place the template on top of a sheet of plastic and trace the shape several times with a sharp-pointed metal scriber. Remove the template and press out the guard. If the scribing was done with enough pressure, the new guard should break easily along the scribed line.

File or sand smooth the edge of the new guard and

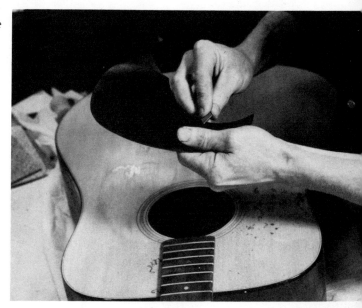

99. Smoothing and beveling top edge with scraper blade

then bevel the top edge all around with a scraper blade. Shave the corner to a tapered edge.

Test the guard in position to make sure it fits properly. If the new shape is larger than the old one, scribe the new shape into the top. Scrape away all the finish from within the gluing area. When the wood is clean, apply the solvent to the back of the guard with a paintbrush. Do not allow any of the solvent to dip over onto the front surface of the guard. Keep brushing out the solvent until the entire area is softened. Stop brushing and wait until the viscous surface begins to dull. Set the guard in the exact position and press it down flat. Roll it out with a small brayer that has a plastic roller, the kind used by paperhangers. Roll out all the air bubbles and continue rolling until total contact is made with the wood.

Place a caul of linoleum or vinyl tile over the guard and weight with a heavy weight. The metal block used in figure 101 weighs 32 pounds. Leave under weight overnight.

Readymade self-adhering pick guards and flamenco tapping plates with a peel-off backing are available from some suppliers. Photographic supply houses also sell large sheets of this same material in different gauges for those who wish to cut their own guard at a fraction of the cost of pre-cuts.

Cut and fit these self-adhering acetate guards before peeling off the backing. The area where they are to be affixed must be spotlessly clean. When the fitting is done and the guard is the right shape, turn it over and across the middle of the guard cut through the backing. Use a sharp razor and be careful not to cut through the acetate. Turn the guard face up and place it in position on the guitar. Tape the top edge of the guard so that the guard is held in position. Lift up the loose end and peel back the lower half of the backing material. As you remove this backing press the acetate down so it will stick. When the lower half has been peeled and stuck fast, remove the tape and do the same with the top half of the guard. Roll out the air bubbles with the brayer when the guard is glued in place.

Self-adhering guards do not stick as well as the solvent-softened acetate guards but can be applied on a finished surface. Solvent-softened guards must be applied to bare wood but can be lacquered over when the guitar is lacquered.

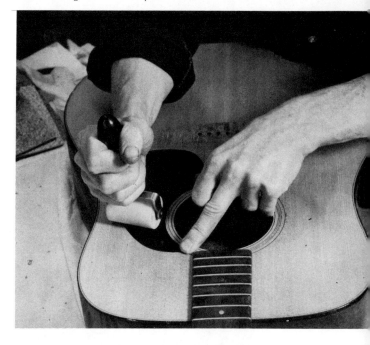

100. Rolling flat with brayer

101. Weighted with 32-pound weight over linoleum caul

Stringed instruments that are precious because of their antiquity and the renown of their makers pose special problems for the restorer. Apart from their intrinsic value as precious artifacts, they are important records of our musical past. Museums, the principal repositories of ancient instruments, go to extraordinary lengths to protect this valuable legacy; humidity is carefully controlled, sealed cases keep out dust particles laden with corrosive impurities, and air-conditioning regulates temperatures and limits gaseous atmospheric impurities such as sulfur dioxide. Even light is controlled to minimize the hazard to organic materials and varnishes from damaging ultraviolet rays.

The primary responsibility of the luthier faced with the restoration of an antique instrument is to arrest, insofar as possible, the process of decay and to accomplish this in a manner that accords with the apparent intention of the maker. The precise intentions of ancient luthiers, unfortunately, are often difficult to know. In the absence of a corroborative body of work as in the case of Stradivarius, restoration becomes a matter of patient research and educated guesswork especially with instruments ravaged by long neglect.

The highest goal of restoration has always been to restore old instruments to a playable condition that faithfully renders the sound their design and construction most clearly ordain. This is particularly true of instruments prized for their musical rather than visual qualities.

On the other hand, guitar makers of the sixteenth to eighteenth centuries were preoccupied with the ornamental possibilities of mother-of-pearl, tortoise shell, and ivory inlay and the lacy intricacies of layered parchment rosettes. *Lutherie* was a testament to the flamboyant virtuosity of magnificent craftsmen but musical quality was secondary.

Restoration of instruments prized for their decorative qualities can be limited to superficial or cosmetic repairs—replacement of lost marquetry and other purely visual elements. Cosmetic repair is frequently the only course possible in situations of advanced decay where the cost of the man hours necessary for extensive restoration is prohibitive. In such cases it is sometimes advisable to build an exact replica rather than undertake major restoration which might prove more difficult and expensive in the long run.

RESTORATION TECHNIQUES for ANTIQUE INSTRUMENTS

103. *Interior of lute showing old repairs*

104. Lifting off rosette with hot knife

105. Scraping away old layer of black paint

Much of the difficulty in restoration work is undoing the crude handiwork of unskilled repairmen. A sad example of this is a guitar-lute made by Mathaeus Stautinger in 1768 and from the collection of the University of Pennsylvania Museum.

The soundboard, obviously a replacement, was made of an inferior grade of soft pine stained a dark brown. The pin bridge (unknown on lutes) was fractured and incorrectly positioned. A pierced and carved rosette excised from an earlier lute was glued in back of the sound hole. Pieces of the rosette were missing and the parchment backing was peeling off. The vaulted back or boat had many small cracks, several cross-grain fractures and some seam separation. A crude coat of black paint covered the boat and a layer of varnish had been applied to the soundboard.

Since the instrument to begin with was not an important one and all claims to antiquity had been so grievously compromised, the curator, Agi Jambor, authorized the reconstruction of the lute for baroque ensemble playing.

Work began with the removal of the black paint. It was so dry and brittle, it came off easily with a small scraper blade. The beautifully flamed curly maple back slowly emerged from under the ugly coat of paint. Painstaking work with a razor blade removed paint from cracks and sunken areas. Scraping was done cautiously to remove only the paint and not the wood.

Before removing the top, a careful tracing was made of the top contour of the lute. The top was removed with a heated knife inserted into the glue joint and slowly worked around the entire perimeter. The rosette was separated in the same manner using the heated knife.

After all the bracing was cut away from the back of the rosette, it was submerged in liquid paint remover to dissolve a heavy coat of varnish. It was cleansed in a bath of turpentine and dried.

A photogram was made of the rosette to record the overall pattern. In a darkroom, the rosette was placed on enlarging paper with a sheet of glass on top to weight it. A 20-second light exposure produced a strong black-and-white negative image of the rosette.

The lost pieces were drawn back in place by making a tracing of an unbroken quarter of the symmetrical design and then superimposing it in register over the missing sections. After gingerly scrap-

106. *Photogram of broken rosette*

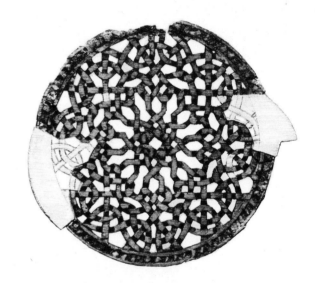

107. *Patched rosette with design penciled in*

108. *Restored rosette glued in place*

ing away the cracked and peeling parchment from the back of the rosette, the back was sanded smooth with some fine sandpaper. A black circle was scribed on a piece of vegetable parchment marking the diameter of the grillwork portion of the rosette. Clear epoxy cement was spread over the circled area in a thin layer and the rosette was set in position and glued. It was left overnight with a weighted board on top of it to ensure good contact.

Protruding fragments were cut away from the broken sections to make a cleaner contour for piecing in new wood. A tracing of the cleaned-up sections was transferred to spruce of the same graining and thickness. The sections were cut so that the grain would all run the same way on the completed rosette. They were glued in place with epoxy and left to dry.

The design pattern was traced onto the new wood grafts and cut out with an Exacto knife. The woven design effect was carved with a fine chisel and then the wood was stained to the color of the rosette. When the rosette was completely whole again, the knife was used to cut away the parchment from all the openings.

Traditionally, the lute rose or rosette is an integral part of the top. The designs were the trademarks of great makers but were frequently copied by other luthiers. Accordingly, a new top of Bavarian spruce was prepared and planed to a thickness of 3/32". Two circles delimiting the borders of the carved border design were incised with a circle cutter and then the center hole was cut out. This hole was sized to the exact diameter of the grillwork portion of the rosette.

The fragmented border of the rosette was cut away along the black circle line with a jeweler's saw. After careful fitting of the rosette to the hole in the new top, it was edge-glued to the hole with polyvinyl glue. The border design was carved to simulate the original design. Except for the age-darkened wood of the rosette surrounded by the pale wood of the new top, the appearance was one of an unbroken surface with a rosette pierced and carved into it.

Bracing of Sitka spruce was glued across the back of the rosette and spruce struts were glued to the back of the soundboard in conformance with traditional practice.

A rosewood bridge in the style of eighteenth-century lutes was fashioned to replace the bogus pin

110. *Knives in electric heater*

111. *New top with characteristic bracing*

109. *Clamping crack with clear plastic caul*

bridge. Calculations based on the first fret space representing $\frac{1}{18}$ of the vibrating string length gave the correct position for the bridge. The bridge was sealed with a wash coat of shellac and glued in position.

Staining wooden instruments is an unacceptable practice in traditional *lutherie*. The beauty of wood was always considered an important aesthetic part of the whole and varnish was employed to accentuate as well as protect this beauty. The problem of the dark rosette and the paler soundboard wood was resolved by masking the rosette and tinting the top with a spray coat of brown spirit varnish over a wash coat of clear shellac. The spirit varnish was close to the color of the rosette and sufficiently tinted the top to give a homogeneous appearance to the entire top.

All the cracks in the boat were glued together with polyvinyl glue and clamped to ensure alignment of both edges while gluing. Strips of parchment were glued over the more serious cracks as added reinforcement. When all the cracks and seam openings

112. Peg shaping machine

113. Gluing on top in jig

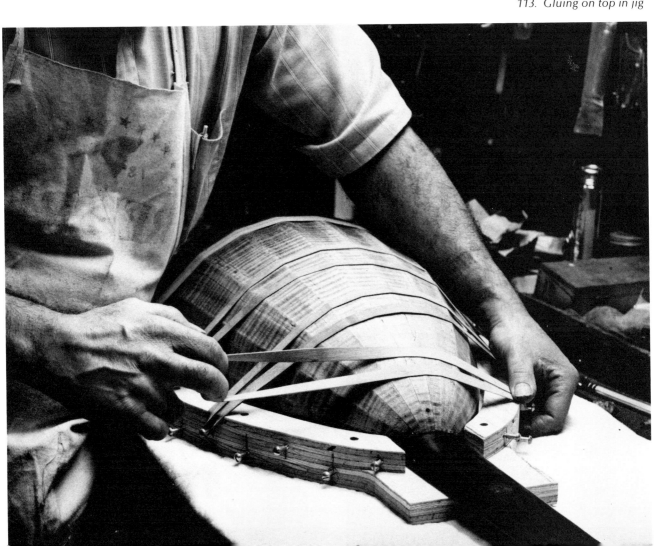

were fixed, the top was jigsawed to the exact shape of the original contour tracing.

The top was fitted to the body and glued on with the aid of a special jig (Fig. 113). A mold was made to the same shape as the top with screws spaced around the outside perimeter of the mold. Hide glue was applied to the lining and edge of the lute and then pressed down onto the soundboard resting in the mold. Rubber bands, stretched between screws and over the boat, provided clamping pressure.

The next day the rubber bands were removed and the edge of the top was sanded flush with the sides. A thin ledge was cut into the top perimeter of the lute with a router and carbide-tipped cutter. A single strip of maple binding was glued into place around the lute.

The tuning peg holes were trued with a tapered reamer and the pegs were carefully rounded and fitted with the aid of a peg shaver.

Three coats of clear varnish, sanded between coats, were applied to the body of the instrument. Final polishing was done with pumice and water.

114. Reaming peg holes

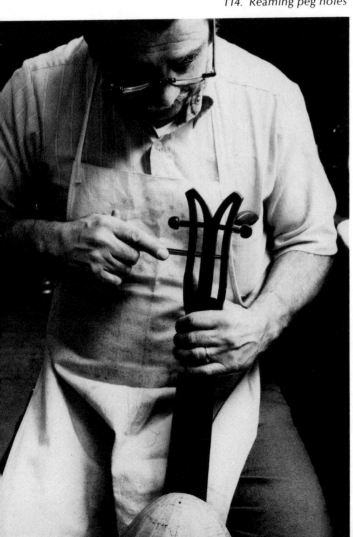

115. Completely restored lute

116. Mandolin sound hole ornamentation with missing inlay

117. Sawing out mother-of-pearl pieces with jeweler's saw

Inlay materials for guitars have included ivory, tortoise shell, mother-of-pearl and the entire range of marquetry woods: rosewood, ebony, holly, maple, satinwood, and others. Replacement of lost inlay is a continuing activity for restorers of old instruments. An Italian mandolin with missing mother-of-pearl (or "pearl" as it is commonly called) pieces presents an example of a typical inlay repair job.

The missing pieces were bedded in a niello-type mixture of fine ebony sawdust mixed with hide glue to a paste consistency and applied after the pearl pieces were glued in place. Portions of the paste had crumbled and the entire paste surface was laced with cracks caused by the complete drying out of the glue binder. Unless such paste fillers are protected by a good film of varnish, the binder eventually loses its plasticity and crumbling results.

A careful tracing was made of one of the remaining pearl pieces and transferred to a thin sheet of stiff paper. The shape was then cut out with a swivel-type stencil-cutting knife. This stencil was taped to a sheet of pearl thinned to the depth of the inlay mortise and sprayed with an aerosol can of orange Acrolite, a water-soluble paint. Enough copies were sprayed to replace all the missing pieces.

A wood board was prepared with a ½" hole drilled near an edge with a narrow exit channel to permit passage of a saw blade. As sawing progressed, the pearl sheet was gradually turned to keep the sawing contour over the hole. This system permits sawing of small parts with the support necessary to keep the pearl from moving while it is being sawed. A jeweler's saw with fine blade is moved up and down in a vertical line and cuts only on the down stroke. Pearl, ivory, and other inlay materials can be safely sawed in this manner. A good supply of saw blades is necessary because they are very fine and break easily.

If final sawing must be done on a small piece that has been cut out, it must be held in a pair of parallel pliers with the pliers resting against some support while sawing is completed. Any movement of the piece during sawing may crack the piece or the blade. Final touch up filing with jeweler's files was accomplished with the pieces held in a parallel pliers.

The inlay mortises were scraped clean with a fine chisel and all the pieces were set in place to check their fit. They were glued in place with Duco cement and clamped.

Fine ebony sawdust and white polyvinyl glue were mixed to a paste consistency in a mortar. The paste was quickly spread over the entire inlay portion of the rosette with a small knife and firmly pressed into all crevices. When thoroughly dry, the area was smoothed with fine garnet paper and subsequently varnished.

An alternate method for transferring the shape of larger pieces of missing inlay is one using heavy aluminum foil instead of tracing paper.

Paper-backed aluminum foil—the kind used for heavily embossed labels—is taped in place over the inlay mortise, shiny face down. The contour of the mortise is pressed into the foil with a ball-ended stylus or other blunt burnishing tool. The foil is lifted and the shape cut out with a small manicure scissors. This cutout is glued to the pearl or ivory with rubber cement and the saw follows the contour. Sawing can also be done by spraying the background, removing the foil cutout, and following the stenciled edge.

118. *Clamping pearl replacements with plastic caul*

REFINISHING

Major refinishing of a guitar begins with stripping of the old finish. Stuff rags into the sound-hole opening to catch drips and remove saddle, nut, and tuning machines if neck is to be refinished. If the bridge and pick guard are not going to be removed, mask them with white masking tape. A rosewood bridge will bleed under the solvent action of paint and varnish remover, and stain a spruce top.

Coat the guitar with a semipaste remover such as Glid-strip. Apply the paste liberally with an old brush. Flow on in an even coat and avoid brushing back and forth. Allow to set for 15 or 20 minutes until the finish begins to soften into a viscous mass. Scrape off the softened finish with a broad spatula. Work the blade carefully to avoid gouging the wood. Apply a second

119. Applying varnish remover

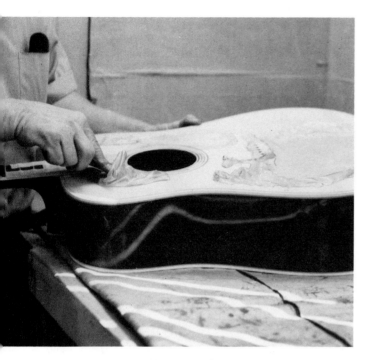

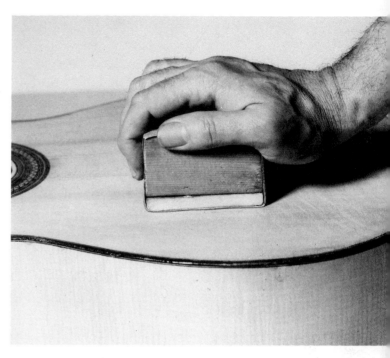

120. Scraping off old finish with putty knife

121. Sanding smooth with felt-backed sanding block

coat if all the old finish has not been removed. Many removers contain paraffin wax to retard evaporation of the solvents, and all traces of this wax must be removed from the wood. When all of the softened sludge has been removed with the spatula, cleanse the surface with a wax solvent such as turpentine or benzine. Do not use water to cleanse the bare surface.

If only a portion of the guitar such as the top or back is to be refinished, mask all adjacent areas with heavy paper and white masking tape.

Clean up the stripped wood with a light sanding with fine flint or garnet paper. Examine the sandpaper to make sure it doesn't clog, a sure sign that the surface has not been entirely stripped clean.

Spruce and maple are close-grain woods and do not have to be filled. Open-pore woods such as rosewood and mahogany must be filled before they can be finished. Removers may pull some of the old filler from the pores and this filler must be replaced. Filler is a mixture of ground silex and color in a varnish-type vehicle and comes in several colors. The color of filler used should be a shade darker than the wood it will fill.

Before filling, coat the area to be refinished with a wash coat of 5-pound cut white shellac reduced 5 parts alcohol to 1 part shellac by volume. Shellac has a shelf life of six to eight months and must be fresh or it will not dry properly. This preliminary wash coat makes the filling operation easier and gives cleaner results. It also stops color changes in the wood by retarding the absorption of oils and resins contained in the filler.

Sand smooth wash-coated areas with another light going-over with fine garnet paper. Use a sanding block made of wood with felt glued to the bottom of the block. The felt slows the buildup of heat caused by friction and the clogging of sandpaper that heat can cause. It also prevents the gouging that can occur when using a sharp-cornered block of wood.

Dig a lump of filler out of the can and thin it with benzine (not benzol) until it has the consistency of heavy cream. Brush it on parallel to the grain with an old paintbrush, working it into the pores. Avoid getting filler onto the spruce soundboard.

When the filler dries to a fogged or cloudy appearance—usually about 20 minutes—wipe off the excess filler with a coarse cloth. Remove the excess by rubbing across the grain with enough pressure to pad

122. *Filling pores with filler mixed to cream consistency*

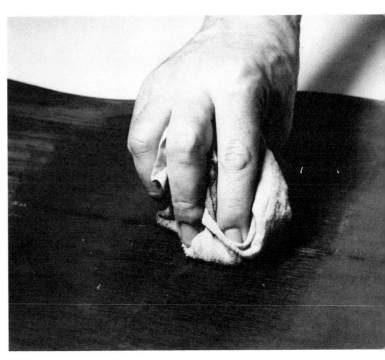

123. *Wiping off dried filler without pulling out filler in pores*

125. *Hanger for suspending guitar while varnishing*

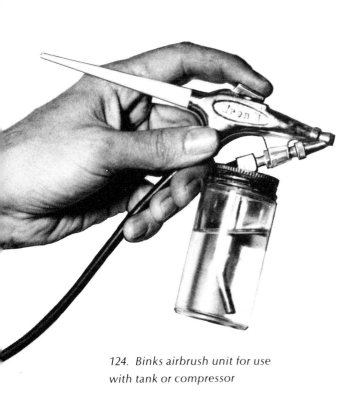

124. *Binks airbrush unit for use with tank or compressor*

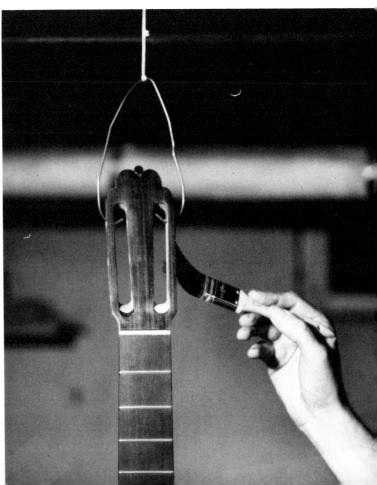

and pack the filler more firmly into the pores. Finish wiping by rubbing parallel to the grain with a soft, lint-free cloth. If the filler is wiped before it is sufficiently dry it will be pulled from the pores; if the filler is too dry, wiping will produce muddy results. Practice and good judgment will yield a professional job. On new wood, filling may have to be done twice to fill all the pores and provide a hard, smooth base for finishing. The final finish can be no better than the surface underneath.

Before any finish is applied to the guitar, the filler must be absolutely dry. Laying varnish or other coating on partially dry filler is a common mistake made in finishing. The final finish will not dry, meaning that all the finishing materials will have to be removed down to the wood, then starting all over again. Allow at least a day, preferably two, for drying filler.

When dry, coat the filled areas with a sealer coat of 2-pound cut shellac made by mixing 1 part alcohol to 1 part 5-pound cut shellac. This can be applied with brush or spray gun. Allow overnight drying before lightly sanding with No. 7/0 paper. When thoroughly dry, shellac will not adhere to sandpaper but will leave a fine white powder on the surface. Gummed up sandpaper means the shellac is inferior or that humidity has slowed the normal drying action. Do *not* sand where lacquer is going to be used over rosewood or dark mahogany.

Sealing is essential on rosewood because rosewood will bleed under lacquer and will also seriously delay the drying of oil varnish. Use only one coat for sealing. Heavy coats of shellac will retard the drying of some lacquers.

Both varnish and lacquer are used to finish guitars. Generally, a good oil varnish will produce a more durable finish than will lacquer. Varnish is also easier to apply by brush; lacquer is usually applied by spray gun.

Good varnishes for musical instruments are sold by violin supply houses. They are available in different shades of gold and brown and drying time is usually at least a day. Quick-drying varnishes are not suitable for musical instruments.

Commercially produced guitars are finished with several coats of sprayed lacquer. When thoroughly dry, final polishing is done with a lambs-wool buffing pad held in an electrically operated polishing unit. A lacquer polishing compound such as Dupont No. 7 auto polishing compound is used with the buffer to produce a high gloss. Dupont No. 7 can be thinned with water for easy use.

Modern lacquers spray well, dry fast, and multiple coats can be applied with good adhesion between coats without the scarifying or dulling required between varnish coats; the solvent in each coat tends to soften the preceding layer, thereby affecting a good bond. Lacquers are water-clear and their visual effect on wood is minimal. Grain and color are intensified but essential color or hue remains unchanged. Lacquer gives a tough abrasion-resistant finish but one with less flexibility than varnish.

Except for the cheapest guitars, stain is not used on guitars. If color-matching requires it, color can be introduced by using sprayed spirit varnish. Violin supply houses sell spirit varnishes in various violin colors and they can be used under lacquer or varnish.

Apply varnish with a soft-hair 1" flagged and tipped brush. Twirl a new brush between your palms to shake out loose hairs. Do not use a varnish brush for anything but varnish.

Work in a well lit, dust-free room and clean off the surface with a tack rag, a rag impregnated with varnish until tacky but not damp. Apply varnish in long, even strokes with a minimum of brushing. When the varnish is dry, sand lightly with fine sandpaper—varnish does not adhere well to a glossy surface. Apply three coats, sanding between each coat. Before applying the fourth and last coat, sand away all bumps caused by dripping and overlaps.

Varnish must dry for two weeks—the longer the better—before being rubbed to its final polished finish. When thoroughly dry, smooth the finish with 400A wet-or-dry silicon carbide paper and water. Dip a folded piece of the paper into water and carefully sand away all lumps and unevenness. Inspect the surface frequently to avoid going through the finish. Be very careful when sanding the edge, the easiest place to go through the finish.

After initial smoothing has been accomplished, change to 600A silicon carbide paper and rub until all surface scratches are eliminated. This rubbing operation softens the varnish and final polishing must be delayed for a few days. Powdered rottenstone and

126. *Professional spray operation (lacquer)*

water rubbed with a felt pad will give a high polish.

Where time is a factor, lacquer is a better choice. Lacquer comes in brush or spray form. Spray lacquers dry too fast for brushing but a brush lacquer can be sprayed. When brushed, lacquer is flowed on with a good-quality soft-haired brush. Load the brush with as much lacquer as it can hold and flow it on in one direction. Sanding between coats is unnecessary.

For spray-gun application of lacquer, pressure must be adjusted to suit the viscosity of the lacquer. Follow the directions of the manufacturer for thinning and application. Use a high-quality thinner to ensure a more trouble-free finish.

Spraying distance is usually about 10″. Too-close spraying can cause sagging or a pebbling effect known as orange peel. Spraying from too far at high pressure can cause a rough, sandy finish. Only experience will produce facility with a spray gun.

If an electric buffing unit is not available, lacquer can be polished to a high gloss with lacquer-polishing compound and a felt pad.

Small areas such as newly splinted or patched wood can be spot-finished with a padding lacquer. These lacquers are formulated to use over bare wood, shellac, varnish, or lacquer finish. They are applied in the manner of French polishing techniques but are much easier to use.

First, all grease and dirt must be removed from the old finish with a dewaxing liquid. A small pad made of lint-free cotton or cheesecloth is shaped to the required size. The pad is dipped into the padding lacquer and then pressed against the palm of the hand to ensure equal dispersion. Room temperature must be at least 65° F.

Move the pad in circular or figure-eight motions, beginning with light pressure and increasing as the pad dries out. Slide the pad on and off the surface without stopping. Resting the pad in one spot will mar the finish. Do not use too much lacquer at one padding, and allow at least an hour between paddings.

Staining colors miscible with French polishes and padding lacquers are sold by H. Behlen & Bro. under the name Match-O-Stain. They also market an excellent padding lacquer under the name Qualasole. The colors are dipped with a Qualasole-moistened pad and applied in the same padding motions. In this way color blending and buildup of finish can be accomplished in a small area.

127. *Buffing to high polish with lamb's-wool buffer and Duco No. 7 auto polish*

SUPPLY SOURCES

A. Constantine & Son, Inc.
2050 Eastchester Rd., Bronx, N. Y. 10461
Supplies, wood, tools. Catalog.

Vitali Import Co.
5944-48 Atlantic Blvd., Maywood, Calif. 90270
Wood, machines, accessories. Catalog.

H. L. Wild Co.
510 E. 11th St., New York, N.Y. 10009
Wood, machines, accessories. Catalog.

Metropolitan Music Co.
222 Park Avenue South, New York, N. Y. 10003
Wood, varnish, tools. Catalog.

Ibex Company
Millerton, N. Y. 12546
Purfling cutter, flip clamps. Catalog.

H. Behlen & Bro. Inc.
Box 698, Amsterdam, N. Y. 12010
All wood finishing materials. Catalog.
(Minimum order $15)

Marina Music
1892 Union Street, San Francisco, Calif. 94123
Wood, tools, accessories. Catalog.

Sherry-Brener, Ltd.
3145 W. 63rd St., Chicago, Ill. 60629
Wood, accessories. Catalog.

Woodcraft Supply Corp.
313 Montvale Avenue, Woburn, Mass. 01801
Highest quality woodworking tools. Catalog.

International Violin Supply Co.
414 E. Baltimore St., Baltimore, Md. 21202
Wood, accessories. Catalog.

J. F. Wallo
1319 "F" Street N.W., Washington, D.C.
Wood, accessories. Catalog.

Flexcraft Industries
527 Avenue "P", Newark, N. J. 07105
#337—clear liquid solvent for adhering acetate
pick guards. (Minimum order $10)

CANADA

Bill Lewis Music Ltd.
3607 W. Broadway, Vancouver 8, B. C.
Wood, accessories. Catalog.

ENGLAND

Sidney Evans Ltd.
49 Berkley Street, Birmingham, BI 2LG, England
Wood, accessories. Catalog.

AUSTRALIA

Perfectus Airscrew
175 Mason Street, Newport, 3015 Victoria
Wood.

Lamberti Bros.
366 Victoria St., North Melbourne, 3061 Victoria
Fret wire, machines.